W9-ABF-869

WITHDRAWN

Studies in German Literature, Linguistics, and Culture

STUDIES IN GERMAN LITERATURE, LINGUISTICS,
AND CULTURE

Editorial Board

Kurt Fickert

End of a Mission:

Kafka's Search for Truth in His Last Stories

CAMDEN HOUSE

Copyright © 1993 by
CAMDEN HOUSE, INC.

Published by Camden House, Inc.
Drawer 2025
Columbia, SC 29202 USA

Printed on acid-free paper.
Binding materials are chosen for strength and
durability.

ISBN: 1-879751-57-7

Library of Congress Cataloging-in-Publication Data

Fickert, Kurt J.
        End of a mission : Kafka's search for truth in his last stories /
Kurt Fickert.
        p. cm. -- (Studies in German literature, linguistics, and
culture)
        Includes bibliographical references and index.
        ISBN 1-879751-57-7 (alk. paper)
        1. Kafka, Franz, 1883-1924--Criticism and interpretation.
I. Title. II. Series: Studies in German literture, linguistics,
and culture (Unnumbered)
PT2621.A26Z68558   1993
833'.912--dc20   93-19361
                                                                          CIP

Contents

Acknowledgments

I WOULD LIKE TO express my gratitude to Chris Fickert, without whose computer knowledgeability my manuscript would never have become fit to print.

K.F.

Introduction

Defining the Ineffable

> *Die Kritik sucht den Wahrheitsgehalt*
> *eines Kunstwerkes, der Kommentar*
> *seinen Sachgehalt.*
>
> Walter Benjamin,
> "Goethes Wahlverwandtschaften"

IN HIS JOURNAL for the year 1917 Franz Kafka expressed in a few words his objective in writing fiction; the entire entry reads: "Temporary satisfaction I can as yet have from works such as 'Country Doctor,' provided that I can still achieve something of that sort (very unlikely). Elation however, only if I can raise the world into (the sphere of) the pure, the true, the immutable."[1a] The passage places Kafka in the company of countless authors who have contributed to the literature of the Western world and similarly claimed to be seekers of truth. To readers and interpreters of Kafka (the terms are interchangeable and therefore redundant) the statement of principle proffered by Kafka presents both an occasion to explore Kafka's concept of truth in literature and an opportunity to study the development of the theme in his work. In this regard it would seem appropriate first of all to consider, at least tangentially, the ideology of "truth" as a philosophic and literary construct.

The very words Kafka used in describing the goal of his literary mission — giving expression to the pure, the true, the immutable — exhibit his orientation to the point of view established in classical Greek philosophy. Kafka's triadic formulation manifestly duplicates Plato's well-known association of the real, the stable, and the unchang-

---

[1] Franz Kafka, *Tagebücher 1910-1923* (Frankfurt am Main: Fischer, 1976), p. 389. Quotations in the original German appear at the end of the respective chapters, designated by alphabetic superscripts. The translations are my own in all cases.

ing with the concept of knowledge.[2] Patently, Kafka's involvement with the writings of the Greek philosophers began in the early years of his schooling in a humanistic *Gymnasium*; Greek and Latin were an essential part of the curriculum. Although Kafka would later in his life disparage his ability to understand and thus put to use the abstractions which prevail in philosophic thought (a self-evaluation with which his lifelong friend and biographer Max Brod concurred), he maintained an interest in the subject to the very end.[3] In their youth he and Brod read Plato's *Protagorus* together, probably by way of translating it. Further evidence of Kafka's continuing interest in Plato's thought is the number of books containing his writings kept in his library.

Notably, the main thrust of Greek philosophy in regard to establishing a premise for that which is true lay in the direction of distinguishing between the actual, the physical or natural world, and the insubstantial world of perception. Thus the axiomatic basis on which the classical concept of truth rested consisted of the insistence that the idea correspond to the actual; i.e., the perception that it is raining is true only if in fact it is raining. The principle that the truth can but be referential fostered the conviction that the function of art was to imitate reality. This precept lent itself particularly well to becoming the rule in regard to literature since it is the only one of the forms of art which is capable of making statements or assertions. Indeed, as has already been observed, writers most often claim that what they profess can be verified.

A striking feature of Kafka's fiction is openly the literalness of the fantastic events with which it deals. He takes great pains, for example, to convince the reader of "Die Verwandlung" ("Metamorphosis" or "The Transformation") that the repulsive insect whose shape the protagonist has assumed truly exists. Kafka achieves verisimilitude in this instance by depicting first the characteristics of the vermin which Gregor Samsa has acquired; then an impartial (if negatively inclined) observer comes on the scene to confirm Gregor's catastrophic suspicions. One by one, the members of the family then attest to the

---

[2] Another such direct connection between Kafka and Plato's work involves Kafka's short prose piece "Bäume" published in *Betrachtung* (*Observation*, 1913, customarily translated too freely as *Meditation*). Kafka's use of the image of trees standing as if unsupported in the snow resembles Plato's well-known depiction of trees reflected in the water in order to symbolize an erroneous perception of reality.

[3] Kafka's inability to deal systematically with philosophic concepts was also attested to officially; as a law student he was required to attend for one semester a course in philosophy and subsequently to pass an oral examination on the subject; he failed the test. See Hartmut Binder, *Kafka-Handbuch* I (Stuttgart: Alfred Kröner, 1979), p. 191.

actuality of his transformation. The sophistication of Kafka's under-girding of the reality he seeks to present in the form of the bizarre can most readily be appreciated by scrutinizing the structure of "In der Strafkolonie" ("In the Penal Colony"). It rests on the confrontation between an advocate of punishment for all infractions of universal law by execution on a deadly machine and another impartial observer, in this case a rational and fair-minded individual. Kafka devotes a seemingly disproportionate number of pages to a description of the machine; thereby it becomes as real as the guillotine and the cross, both of which it resembles. In addition, the fervor of the officer of the execution who defends using the machine and the dispassionate reasoning of the spectator who is finally forced to reject it and the purpose it serves lend credence to the existence of such an instrument. Kafka's careful bolstering of the reader's credulity so that that which he has created as a symbol, as a figure of speech, will take on the form of fact also has the function of dealing with another aspect of fulfilling the requirements for a truthful statement. It must be not only referenti-ally true but also totally so; in this context the insect cannot turn out to have been a figment of Gregor's imagination or the execution machine a vision in a nightmare. In regard to the classical version of the concept of truth, all statements are literal or they are false. Consequently in aspiring to reveal the inalterable truth through a work of fiction, Kafka must follow his presentation of fact with a thorough testing of its substantiality. Thereby, in all of Kafka's longer stories, the "plot" consists of an attempt on the part of the protagonist to verify the authenticity of the calamity which has befallen him. In "Das Urteil" ("The Judgment"),[4] for instance, Georg Bendemann proves that his perception of his father's omnipotence and his own unworthiness is valid by carrying out the sentence of self-execution his father has pronounced. In Kafka's novels the motif of checking the reliability of the premise on which the story rests constitutes the spring activating the series of events it portrays; K.'s conviction that he has been called to the castle in that narrative is put to the test in a seemingly endless fashion. Beda Allemann has identified this stylistic feature as "that structural characteristic of Kafka's works which may be described as a continuous modifying and retracting of what at first seemed an absolutely positive statement and what at last turns out to have been

---

[4] In the light of Kafka's mission to present reality through words, the fact that "Urteil" becomes "ordeal" in the English language should be of interest, whether or not he was aware of the relationship.

a mere hypothesis."[5] In seeking accuracy, Kafka's writing itself marked by way of the growing meticulousness of his symbolism his progress in his search for truth.

Although the concept of truth based on its referential character which classical Greek philosophy had established continued to be accepted through the centuries, its relevance, particularly in the rapidly developing field of aesthetics, was more and more to be subjected to challenge. The Romantic movement in the arts brought about a radical change in thinking on the subject of the very nature of the work of art; the contention was made and supported that as a product of the imagination its validity did not rest on its correspondence to the actual world. As a progenitor of criteria in German letters Goethe championed the cause of a definition of truth in literature which emphasized its inner and individual point of origin. In his *Maximen und Reflexionen* he posited: "If I know my relationship to myself and my environment, I call that (knowing) the truth. And thus everyone can have his or her own truth, and yet it will be the same (truth)."[b] It is more than evident that Kafka was well acquainted with Goethe's work and held it in high esteem. Of note in regard to Kafka's ambition to evoke the pure, the true, the immutable in his fiction is the coincidence of this triadic ideal with Goethe's aim to achieve "Dauer im Wechsel" ("the immutable in the changeable"). Goethe's often-quoted injunction "Stirb und werde" ("die and become," perhaps, more expressly, "die *to* become") is a rewording of the message and pertains particularly, if in a roundabout fashion, to the prevalence of the motif of transformation which is rife in Kafka's narratives. This inner-directed literary vantage point runs counter to the widely accepted philosophic dogma that truth of any kind must have an external point of reference. Consequently, the concept of inner or aesthetic truth came into prominence as an alternative view which flourished during Kafka's lifetime.

The amalgamation of the literal — Kafka's at times oppressive realism — and the imaginative — his excursions into the realm of the fantastic — was augmented in the course of his literary career; then, also, Kafka's perception of the goal he sought to reach in his writing underwent a change in the direction of finding a purpose of greater subtlety and wider scope. What, it would seem, he aspired to express in his early work, which reached a pinnacle with the "breakthrough" story "Das Urteil" ("The Judgment") and a slightly lower one with "Die Verwandlung," was the truth about familial relationships. In a

---

[5] Beda Allemann, "Metaphor and Antimetaphor" in *Interpretation: The Poetry of Meaning*, ed. Stanley Romaine Hopper and David L. Miller (New York: Harcourt, Brace and World, 1967), p. 111.

relevant and perspicacious article Walter H. Sokel has analyzed the relationship between language and truth in Kafka's narratives; he avers that Kafka held a dichotomous view of life even in his early years. On the one hand, he confronted the real world, having at its core the activities of family, community and occupation; on the other, he tried to fulfill his obligations to the immaterial world of literature. Although at first he tended to regard the material side of life as more substantive and attempted to incorporate his writing in the mundane sphere of life, he came gradually to look upon the world of literature (language) as separate and superior and to develop a sense of mission in respect to it. Sokel summarizes: "Living in and as literature, Kafka felt as close as anyone could to that unity which he called truth."[6] To reach this high goal, however, Kafka began to realize that there must be a shift in emphasis; by degrees he placed the referential, mimetic elements in his fiction farther in the background. As Sokel proposes, Kafka gave precedence to developing "a very special kind of non-referential, merely allusive language (to create) a means by which human beings may receive an inkling of the invisible, true world."[7]

In concentrating on the "purity" of his prose instead of its scientific exactness, Kafka was in accord with the poetics espoused by a community of artists and theoreticians who, spurning realism and naturalism, ushered in the modernist age at the turn of the century. The literary circle in Prague with which Kafka was affiliated eagerly adhered to the literary precepts of the French symbolists and their German counterparts. Stefan George and Hugo von Hofmannsthal, whose work advanced the position that the criterion for perfection in the arts, considered to be a kind of truth, was the extent to which they achieved the beautiful, exerted a considerable influence on Kafka's thinking. This linking of truth and beauty as a creed in aesthetics was celebrated by Keats in a verse from his poem "Ode on a Grecian Urn": "'Beauty is truth, truth beauty,' — that is all Ye know on earth, and all ye need to know." Notably, Keats' theme here in his evocation of figures on a vase which existed only in his imagination was his insistence that the arts lend permanence, immutability, to that which, in reality, is subject to decay. Even decay itself could be raised to the level of the beautiful as, e.g., George's "Komm in den totgesagten Park und schau" ("Come into the park called dead and look about") reveals. The pairing, indeed the absorption of the one concept by the other

---

[6] Walter H. Sokel, "Language and Truth in the Two Worlds of Franz Kafka," *The German Quarterly*, 52:3 (May, 1979), 377.

[7] Sokel, "Language and Truth," p. 375.

became an issue of contention among theoreticians, if not among artists themselves. On the one hand, the Viennese philosopher Friedrich Kainz, whose lectures on aesthetics were delivered in the first decade of the twentieth century, maintained: "The 'artistic truth' which is demanded of an art-work is in no way identical with genuine truth; it is only a metaphor which is misleading in its figurativeness."[8] Contrarily, the philosophic and psychological tenets formulated somewhat earlier in the Austrian capital by Franz Brentano and promulgated by his student Edmund Husserl (among others) maintained that the intellect, and not the world external to it, was the arbiter of reality and that the mind intuitively gave shape and color to objects existing outside of it. It is significant that Kafka attended and presumably participated in the meetings of a Brentano group (they also discussed the aesthetic theories of other philosophers and critics). Although it is clear that Kafka was knowledgeable about the great variety of often conflicting opinions about the arts which were continually being voiced, the extent to which they had an effect on his thinking and his work, or if they impressed him in any way at all, remains a matter of speculation. There is no evidence, for example, that Kafka took note of the ruminations of Fritz Mauthner on the subject of the inadequacy of language to express the true meaning of sensations or perceptions; however, a very similar point of view patently appears in Kafka's letters and journals. This conviction on Kafka's part may more readily have been bolstered by his presumed familiarity with Hugo von Hofmannsthal's Lord Chandos letter. In the same vein, the conjectural nature of the influence on Kafka of the then current philosophical and theoretical literature is strikingly represented by the controversy, as yet unabated, over the dominance of Nietzschean thought in his work. Patrick Bridgwater's study *Kafka and Nietzsche* which finds Nietzsche's influence everywhere in the Kafka canon has been considered most skeptically by Reinhold Grimm who argues that, despite similarities in their writings, the philosopher and the writer are more kindred spirits than master and pupil.[9] In his article Grimm takes into account the fact that both authors have professed to be seekers of the truth and, at the same time, bemoaned its unattainability. Grimm concludes his discussion of the risk involved in making assumptions too readily about Kafka's leaning on Nietzsche's arm with the statement that the topic of truth they addressed

---

[8] Friedrich Kainz, *Aesthetics the Science*, trans. Herbert M. Schueller (Detroit: Wayne State University Press, 1962), p. 81.

[9] See Reinhold Grimm, "Comparing Kafka and Nietzsche," *The German Quarterly*, 52:3 (May 1979), 339-350.

was not theirs but belonged and still belongs in the literary public domain.

However Kafka acquired the conviction that his objective in writing was to reveal the pure, the true, the immutable, the concept of artistic truth may be presumed to have played a part in his arriving at this formulation. In maintaining that he aspired to disclose the deeper meanings he believed to be hidden in everyday experience, obtainable through an intuitive kind of knowing, Kafka placed himself, figuratively speaking, of course, in the company of recent theorists. (It may well be said that Kafka outdistanced history in the literary as well as in the psychosocial realm.) In a summary statement which precedes his study of the evolution of the concept, titled *Die Wahrheit der Dichter* (*Literary Truth*), Wolfgang Kayser posits: "Literature and truth are not opposites, but overlap each other, as upper-level truth, manifest only in (the work's) configuration, and as lower-level truth or believability in regard to the actual."[10c] This commonsensical definition, combining two kinds of truth, a referential kind with an intrinsic and intuitive one, is more descriptive than it is enlightening. Although it would pertain, by and large, to Kafka's early stories in which he portrays credibly both the familiar and the fantastic, it falls short of explaining the multilayered structure of Kafka's later narratives. It is not to be gainsaid that in "Metamorphosis" (or "The Transformation") Kafka intends to depict a true-to-life situation, as it happens, in regard to his own family, and at the same time to express the meaningfulness or truth of the situation by means of a grotesque but exact symbol. In stories written in 1917, in his so-called middle period, such as "Ein Landarzt" ("A Country Doctor"), however, the factual element — the physician's point of view — is so overwhelmed by the extraordinary and imaginative — the groom, horses, wound, etc. — that the point of this commingling is obscured. Here Kayser's explanation would not be particularly helpful. In the case of "Ein Hungerkünstler" ("A Hunger Artist"), one of Kafka's last works, the symbolic can no longer be distinguished from the real or the lower-level from the upper-level truth.

The goal which Kafka set for himself in evoking the pure, the true, the immutable through his fiction requires a more profound analysis than that of Kayser. As a critical discourse on the general topic Albert Hofstadter's *Truth and Art* leaves little, if any room for the external world in the citadel of art. Art, he proposes unabashedly, is non-referential: "Art is, first, intuition. Intuition is the act of imagina-

---

[10] Wolfgang Kayser, *Die Wahrheit der Dichter* (Hamburg: Rowohlt, 1959), p. 8.

tion, prior to any ascription of existence or non-existence to its object."[11] Also emphasizing the inner nature of creativity and accomplishment in the field of the arts but reaching his conclusions more systematically than Hofstadter does, Hans-Georg Gadamer in his treatise *Truth and Method* first takes a stand on the question of whether or not truth and beauty are identical. He maintains: "Where art rules, it is the laws of beauty that are in force and the frontiers of reality are transcended. It is the 'ideal kingdom', which is to be defended against all limitation, even against the moralistic guardianship of state and society."[12] The equivalency of truth and beauty constitutes a key factor in Gadamer's thinking; thus he asserts: "When we understand a text, what is meaningful in it charms us just as the beautiful charms us."[13] According to Gadamer, the message or meaning of a literary work of art only becomes evident after "its context of life, and the religious or secular function which gave it its significance" has been erased. What remains after this process of purification is, in Gadamer's terminology, knowledge, the vessel through which truth is transmitted. It is essential that this kind of knowledge not be mistaken for the imparting of information; rather, it represents "a mode of self-under-standing."[14] Seen in the light of its timelessness, its immutability, human experience, which can be comprehended through self-aware-ness, affords insights on the level of wisdom which have aptly been described as depth meanings. I hold that the uniqueness and durability

[11] Albert Hofstadter, *Truth and Art* (New York & London: Columbia University Press, 1965), p. 40. Offering a similar viewpoint, but one expressed with more restraint, Eliot Deutsch in *On Truth: An Ontological Theory* (Honolulu: The University Press of Hawaii, 1979) first defines imagination: "Imagination is an opening of the mind to reality; it is an act of appropriating experience and, through the appropriation, of overcoming one's estrangement from it" (p. 28). Subsequently, Deutsch takes up the subject of truth in art: "A work of art is true when and only it attains authenticity through the presentation of its own intentionality" (underscored, p. 38).

[12] Hans-Georg Gadamer, *Truth and Method* (New York: Seabury Press, 1975, trans. from the 1965 edition of *Wahrheit und Methode*), p. 74.

[13] Gadamer, *Truth and Method*, p. 446. Hofstadter also proposes that truth and beauty are the same with this contention: "The ultimate aim of aesthetics as a philosophical discipline is to think the truth of art" (*Truth and Art*, p. 51).

[14] Rene Wellek and Austin Warren in their analytical *Theory of Literature* seem to me to provide a clear and succinct statement of the difference between the two kinds of knowledge: "There are two basic types of knowledge, each of which uses a language system of signs: the sciences, which use the 'discursive' mode, and the arts, which use the 'presentational.' Are these both truth? The former is what philosophers have ordinarily meant, while the latter takes care of religious 'myth' as well as poetry," *Theory of Literature* (New York: Harcourt, Brace, 1956), p. 23.

of Kafka's work are related to the perception of his critics and readers that it contains not so much a richness of narrative event or (except for, possibly, *Amerika* or *One Who Vanished*) a Dickensian panoply of characters, but for its depiction of an impassioned quest for certitude in a world completely bereft of it. This study of Kafka's search for truth or meaningfulness in his life and times which he pursued with a sense of mission, especially in his maturity, presupposes that the concept of truth in literature is a valid one. It cogency rests on the fact that even the most esoteric of artistic productions, such as John Cage's presentation of silence as a form of music, has a secure relationship to reality. Thus, too, in "science fiction," no matter how fantastic a shape they assume, animate beings or things can but have the limitations or capacities of the (human) mind which conceived them. Therefore, some vestige of the classical Greek premise that truth must be referential in character as yet remains in place. In other words, the agreement between perception, the mental image, and circumstances in a realm independent of and external to it, is still a factor in an author's achieving the required semblance of veracity. However, from the vantage point of post-Romantic theories of aesthetics this element in the composition of a literary work has lost much of its significance. Kingsley B. Price in his article "Is There Artistic Truth?" makes the point: "The conclusion is that truth, in the correspondence sense, can not function as a criterion for aesthetic excellence."[15] Replacing referentiality as the keystone in establishing the authenticity (meaningfulness) of a fictional work is in recent times both the coherence of the parts with the whole and the forcefulness of the imaginative transformation of the experience on which the fiction is based. The purpose which the reformation (after, as some critics would assert, an initial process of deconstruction) of this self-knowledge serves is to catch up the ineffable in a net of words. Without resorting to the use of a figure of speech, Louis Arnaud Ried has summed up his findings after considering the relationship between art, truth, and reality with this statement: "The aesthetic ... is a basic and irreducible form of *knowledge*" (my italics).[16] In dealing with the stories Kafka wrote in the last years of his life and literary career, I seek to qualify the intimations of mortality he presents or, more simply and directly put, to ferret out at least some of the answers he has concealed in the enigmas of his narratives. I shall account for my offering yet another

[15] Kingsley B. Price, "Is There Artistic Truth?" in *Contemporary Studies in Aesthetics*, Francis J. Coleman, ed. (New York et al.: McGraw-Hill, 1968), p. 277.

[16] Louis Arnaud Ried, "Art, Truth and Reality" in *Aesthetics in the Modern World*, Harold Osborne, ed. (New York: Weybright & Takley, 1968), p. 72.

study of Kafka to add to the thousands which have already appeared by way of a quotation from Gadamer. In the preface to his *Truth and Method* he states categorically: "That truth is experienced through a work of art that we cannot obtain in any other way constitutes the philosophic importance of art, which asserts itself against all reasoning."[17]

In trying to provide additional insights into Kafka's stories, principally those he wrote in the last creative period of his life, this study will make its claims in the light of two reservations or literary caveats. One pertains to a consideration of the fact, some aspects of which have already been alluded to above, that Kafka himself did not make clear the extent to which various theoretical viewpoints affected his poetics, in the strict sense of the word. In an article on the subject of Kafka's poetic creed, Sokel proposes that it was not inflexible; he maintains: "Beside the visionary element in his work there is in his art also a very perceptible striving for clarity and comprehensibility, for the rational in the broadest sense of the word which serves neither self-dissolution nor self-argumentation, but self-perdurability."[18d] Even if Kafka did not espouse the cause of a particular school of philosophic or literary opinion, he set a rigid standard for himself to adhere to in his writing, and, as an ultimate act of faith in the validity of his own judgment, consigned to oblivion at the hands of his literary executor all but a meager amount of his work, both published and unpublished.

Another aspect of Kafka's pursuit of truth in his fiction which must be considered with some circumspection has at its core the difference between his own evaluations and interpretations of his work, when they are at hand, and those of contemporary and later critics. Although due attention must be paid to Kafka's remarks — they are often surmises — in letters and journals about the narratives, fables, sketches, and epigrams themselves, his comments, together with a preponderance of the biographical data, have as of late become peripheral in determining the meaningfulness of his fiction. Wherever Kafka has achieved his objective of raising literature to the heights of the pure, the true, the immutable, he has indeed freed it from its ties to passing circumstance. In turn he has left his work open to a

---

[17] Gadamer, *Truth and Method*, p. xii f.

[18] Walter H. Sokel, "Zur Sprachauffassung und Poetik Franz Kafkas," in *Themen und Probleme*, Claude David, ed. (Göttingen: Vandenhoeck & Ruprecht, 1980), p. 44. Sokel also writes that Kafka's poetics cannot shed light on the unique power (*Wirkungskraft*) of his work. The question arises: If his literary goals are not pertinent to adjudging its value, then why explore them?

continuing process of interpretation, the search for deeper meanings, a kind of knowledge equated with truth. Gadamer has established the validity of studying literature to this end; he states: "It is true that what a thing (work of art) has to say, *its intrinsic content*, first appears only after it is divorced from the fleeting circumstances of its actuality.... But the discovery of the true meaning of a text or a work of art is never finished."[19] It is the lasting achievement of Franz Kafka that much of his writing has merited the phenomenal amount of reinterpretation it has undergone.

---

[19] Gadamer, *Truth and Method*, p. 265 (my italics). A previous statement in this section of Gadamer's book attests to his conviction that, in regard to literature, interpretation is a continuing process: "Every age has to understand a transmitted text in its own way.... The real meaning of a text, as it speaks to the interpreter, does not depend on the contingencies of the author and whom he originally wrote for" (p. 263).

Notes

a. "Zeitweilige Befriedigung kann ich von Arbeiten wie 'Landarzt' noch haben, vorausgesetzt, daß mir etwas Derartiges noch gelingt (sehr unwahrscheinlich). Glück aber nur, falls ich die Welt ins Reine, Wahre, Unveränderliche heben kann."

b. "Kenne ich mein Verhältnis zur mir selbst und zur Außenwelt, so heiß ich's Wahrheit. Und so kann jeder seine eigene Wahrheit haben, und es ist doch immer dasselbige."

c. "Dichtung und Wahrheit sind nun keine Gegensätze, sondern überlagern sich als höhere, nur in der Gestaltung ahnbare Wahrheit, und als niedere Wahrheit oder Glaubwürdigkeit im Sachlichen."

d. "Neben dem visionären Element gibt es in seiner Kunst auch ein sehr deutliches Streben nach Klarheit und Verstehen, nach dem im weitesten Sinne Rationalen, das weder der Selbstauflösung noch der Selbststeigerung, sondern der Selbsterhaltung dient."

1

Accountability

THE REFERENCE IN Kafka's pronouncement of his literary goal to his story "Ein Landarzt" ("A Country Doctor")[1] has a twofold significance. It sets the narrative itself apart as worthy of special recognition and yet places a limit on the amount of approbation it can be afforded. Thereby the account of the country doctor's failed attempt to fulfill his obligations to his patients and community, resulting in two calamities, positions Kafka on the way to reaching literary heights, but not yet at the pinnacle. As the title story in a collection of fourteen "brief narratives" (*kleine Erzählungen*), "Ein Landarzt" has special significance for that reason and despite the fact that Kafka has placed it second in his studied positioning of the lot; he insisted that his publisher follow the order he had established exactly. It is equally noteworthy that he first proposed naming the collection *Verantwortung*; I would choose *Accountability* for this title rather than *Responsibility*, which is also apropos and, perhaps, comes more readily to mind. The German root "verantworten" is the equivalent of "to answer for" (or vice versa). The assumption must be made that Kafka was dealing in these narratives at least to some extent with the theme of justification — not a new one in his work. The substitution of *Ein Landarzt* for *Verantwortung* most probably represents an acknowledgment of the importance this story held for him. The revised title also retains some trace of the abstractness of the earlier one since "ein Landarzt" has the aura of the general, the non-specific, the mythic. Of some consequence here is the difference in the nature of these and earlier titles, to the extent that Kafka himself provided them.[2] Previously Kafka has indicated by way of the use of the definite article a certain limited applicability: "*Das*

---

[1] There is a slight element of ambiguity in this reference since it could pertain as well to the entire collection of stories to which it lent its name.

[2] Since it is apparent that Kafka was most discriminative in selecting his titles, it becomes necessary first of all to establish that he and not Max Brod, who on a number of occasions had to name untitled (and usually unfinished) work, provided them. As an example of the confusion which might arise in assuming that Kafka must be the (chapter) title's supplier, "Das Naturtheater von Oklahoma" has the ring of his terminology, but in fact Brod named the chapter as well as the book, calling it *Amerika* even though he was aware that Kafka used the working title of *Der Verschollene* (*One Who Vanished*).

Urteil," "*Die* Verwandlung," *Der Verschollene, Der Prozeß*. The protagonist's experience in these stories would seem to be on the level of the
personal and individual, while that of *a* (that is, any) country doctor
would have the significance of the general or typical. A number of the
narratives in *Ein Landarzt* have titles of the same non-specific sort: "Ein
Bericht für eine Akademie" ("A Report for an Academy"), "Ein
Traum" ("A Dream"), "Ein Brudermord" ("A Fratricide"), "Eine
kaiserliche Botschaft" ("An Imperial Message"), "Ein Besuch im
Bergwerk" ("A Visit to a Mine"), and "Ein altes Blatt" ("A Page from
an Old Chronicle"). Only in "Ein Landarzt" and "Ein Bericht für eine
Akademie," which has the distinction of being the last in the series,
does the narrator let the principal figure play a somewhat individual-
ized role.

Perhaps the fact that Kafka had an uncle who actually was a
country doctor and, as he well knew, a conscientious one, caused him
to make his protagonist in "Ein Landarzt" an individual rather than a
prototype, at least in the opening pages. The key factor in the doctor's
personality is the fervor of his dedication to his profession. He is both
proud of his devotion to his work and fretful about his shortcomings,
the limits of the healing art. The story begins on this note: "I was very
much disconcerted" ("Ich war in großer Verlegenheit").[3] The doctor's
frustration has come about because he has a very sick patient to visit
but no means by which he can journey to him. On the symbolic level
this situation pertains not only to the one specific physician but to all
physicians; they have, from an idealistic point of view, entered the
profession to cure the sick and yet, in practice, must confront their
inability to carry out their mission fully. Notably, Kafka has here once
again given his fiction a realistic framework; not only has he established the validity of his statement by introducing the pronoun "I,"
thus paying tribute to the narrator's accountability, but he has also
depicted the doctor in a true-to-life quandary. At the same time, by
presenting a typical physician, he has established the possibility of
affording the story a mythic reading.

This widening of the narrative's horizons, its propensity to develop
deeper meanings, becomes evident with startling suddenness. With the
return of the doctor's servant (and companion) Rosa, who has failed
to obtain a means of transportation, a horse, for him, the story takes
a turn toward the bizarre. In his frustration the country doctor kicks
in the door to an unused pigsty and admits the fantastic, the fairytale
world, into his everyday world. Symbolic figures, literary creations,

---

[3] Franz Kafka, *Erzählungen* (Frankfurt am Main: Fischer, 1976), p. 112. Further references to pagination will be given in the text and/or end notes and are to this edition.

emerge from the animal shelter: an imperious stablehand or groom, followed by two strong horses that he commands as "Brother" and "Sister." Rosa tries to convince the doctor that he is still in control of the situation by belittling the significance of the apparitions: "One just doesn't know what all one keeps in supply in his own house."[a] The jesting soon ends when the groom, coming close to Rosa, bites her on the cheek. At exactly this point in the story, Kafka abandons the use of the past tense in his narrative and continues his report in the present. With this device Kafka would seem to want to emphasize the juxtaposition of two worlds, the real and the imaginative, the realm in which truth is referential and the realm in which it is poetic or aesthetic. In the next story in the *Landarzt* collection, "Auf der Galerie" ("In the Theater-Gallery"), a very short piece of fiction, Kafka uses a similar technique in separating reality from fantasy; the true situation is depicted in the subjunctive, contrary-to-fact mode, the imagined situation in the indicative. This device achieves the effect of making more poignant the disconcertion of the protagonist.

The doctor's confusion in confronting the double aspect of reality has at its core the author's — Kafka's — confusion in trying to find his way toward the literary goal he has set for himself in his work. On the symbolic level, Kafka has juxtaposed in "Ein Landarzt" the physician's dilemma in lacking the means or misusing the means to bring about the healing he has sworn to effect and the writer's dilemma in discovering the inadequacy of language in conveying truth or meaning. The question posed by Kafka at the beginning of the story is whether or not fiction, portrayed by the fantastic figures of the horses and their implacable groom, etc., can serve to express the purport of a meaningless life. In an article on the theme of vocation (*Berufung*) in Kafka's work, Malcolm Pasley singles out the country doctor as an example of a character in Kafka's narratives who is committed to carrying out a mission entailing great responsibility; Pasley states: "The theme of the story is thus a man's (real or mistaken) commissioning with a task that lies beyond the province of physical medicine."[4] By accepting the services of the unearthly groom and horses, Kafka's physician chooses to undertake an assignment which seems to consist of healing a mortally ill patient but which actually concerns affirming the significance of art, specifically literature, as a measure of the meaningfulness of human life. The story of "Ein Landarzt" involves primarily the testing of art's validity.

---

[4] Malcolm Pasley, "Kafka and the Theme of 'Berufung'" in *Oxford German Studies*, 9 (1978), 140.

Abandoning his responsibility for Rosa's welfare by turning his back on her plight as the stablehand's victim, the doctor finds himself magically transported to his patient's bedside. He is a youthful figure, lying naked under the covers, watched over by a solicitous family — mother, father, and sister. His first words, "Doctor, let me die" ("Doktor, laß mich sterben"), might cause the physician to infer that his patient is reassuring him that the call for his services had been an urgent one. Other than quite incidentally, the term of address the young man uses would be equally appropriate in talking to an attorney, such as Kafka himself.[5] Despite this plea, or better, because of it, the doctor begins to reassess his situation.

His indecision at this point underscores the story's symbolic significance since it is obviously not the physician who hesitates to stay with his patient. The boy or young man in the bed symbolizes for the author an aspect of himself. In a biographical context, Kafka finds himself in the boy in his relationship to his own family. The problem with which Kafka has dealt in his fiction in the previous period of his writing has revolved around his double life, playing both the only son of a convention-bound businessman and his chosen role of renegade, a practitioner of literature. In "Ein Landarzt" he returns to depicting this dichotomous state of affairs, but with a difference. The doctor's patient is not an outcast; rather, he is tenderly cared for by his family. His father, in particular, makes every effort to cajole the doctor into giving his son a rigorous examination; he offers the physician a glass of the rum he himself drinks only on special occasions. His daughter takes the doctor's coat and brings him a chair. In describing this situation, Kafka has created a version of the truth which runs exactly contrary to the version expressed in his fiction; patently in "Die Verwandlung," for instance, the son Gregor Samsa deteriorates physically while no one in his family seriously considers sending for a doctor. The physician in "Ein Landarzt" concludes that his patient needs only to be kicked out of his bed so that he will come to his senses, and renounces his devotion to the art of healing which has led

---

[5] In a striking juxtaposition of fiction and fact, Kafka reveals in one of his first letters to Milena Jesenská, whom he became acquainted with in 1920, that he had been addressed as "Herr Doktor" (in Czech) by a maid on a momentous occasion; she had come to clean up his room and had found traces of the hemorrhage he had suffered in the previous night. She had told him, "You're not going to last very long." See Franz Kafka, *Letters to Milena*, trans. and intro. Philip Boehm (New York: Schocken Books, 1990), p. 6. The hemorrhage had convinced Kafka that he was seriously ill with tuberculosis. What is truly remarkable about this sequence of events is the consideration that Kafka wrote "Ein Landarzt" before the hemorrhage occurred. Kafka also held himself to have been prophetic in having given the patient in the story a fatal wound.

him to undertake a journey into a world of fantasy. "I am no savior of the world...," he tells himself. "I have (only) been engaged by the district and carry out my obligations to their logical extent, to the point that they get to be almost too much for me."[b]

About to abandon the mission he has set out on, the doctor consoles himself with the thought that he will now at least be able to rescue Rosa. "I must still take care of Rosa; then I'll give the boy his due and go die," he proposes.[c] Representing at this juncture the doctor's (and, of course, Kafka's) accountability to the world of reality, Rosa, long the reliable mediator between her employer and his constituency, alone can provide him with the security, the self-assurance, he needs in dealing with his dichotomous way of life. (They have laughed together at the sight of the magical horses.) In the light of the fact that Kafka has openly associated the figure of his sometime fiancée Felice Bauer with characters in his fiction, e.g., with Frieda Brandenfeld in "Das Urteil," it can readily be assumed that at least a shadow of Felice remains in Kafka's characterization of Rosa. Although the personal, biographical element seems to have been curtailed here, Rosa's presence as a symbol for the perfect muse and/or companion for the dedicated artist-savior gains in stature. As narrator (as well as protagonist) the doctor might well have Rosa and her conciliatory function in mind when he remarks: "Writing prescriptions is easy, but beyond that getting along with people is hard."[d]

Together with "Rosa," the word "schreiben" (to write) can be regarded at this juncture in the story as the pivot on which the action begins to turn, suddenly and dramatically. Having decided without much ado that Rosa can no longer be saved, the doctor all but inexplicably determines to take up again the burden of the over-whelming responsibility he feels he has to his profession. He sets about examining his patient anew and finds below his waist in the region of his hip a large and bloody wound. Kafka's description of this scarlet, worm-infested abscess has offended readers and critics alike.[6] Its ugliness tends to conceal its relationship to art, the realm of the beautiful, even the deadly kind, and its pertinence as another instance of Kafka's fondness for the paradoxical. Equally noteworthy in regard to Kafka's use of wound symbolism is his interest in and appreciation of neoromanticist tropes which transport images of death and decay to the sphere of the artistically beautiful. (As a forerunner of the neoromanticist movement, the poet August, Graf von Platen, wrote, in

---

[6] Gregory Triffitt deems this episode to be "one of the most elusive and repulsive Kafka ever wrote," *Kafka's 'Landarzt' Collection* (New York, etc.: Peter Lang, 1985), p. 134.

the nineteenth century, these prototypal lines: "He whose eyes have beheld beauty,/ Has already committed himself to death.")[e] The artist as a Saint Sebastian figure looms large in this frame of reference. At another point later in the story Kafka describes how some people, presumably the chosen few, obtain the wound: "Created by two blows of an axe at an acute angle. Many offer (lay bare) their flank and (yet) scarcely hear the axe in the woods, let alone its drawing nearer to them."[f] Kafka has left little room for doubt that the sickness of the youngster, made evident by the wound, his suffering, closely resembles that of the artist, specifically the writer, Kafka himself.

In the case of the country doctor, however, there is resistance to the idea of becoming victim to those in his community who look to him for healing in the sense of redemption. The artist as scapegoat, another facet of the Saint Sebastian symbol, now comes upon the scene; it is particularly significant that, at this point, Kafka allows the relationship between the boy and his family, the biographical or autobiographical element in "Ein Landarzt" to fade into the background. The doctor begins to believe that his fate rests in the hands of a wider social group. "That's the way people are in this region," he laments, "always expecting the impossible of a physician."[g] He associates the healing that the community requires him to accomplish with the redemptive kind of healing undertaken by the church. He has, he feels, been made to replace the priest whose faith all have forsaken. Despite his wariness, he chooses to accept the role foisted on him by all of humanity. Resignedly, he announces: "Well, whatever you want: I did not volunteer; if you (want to) use me for spiritual purposes, I'll let even that happen to me; how could I expect anything better, old doctor (that I am), robbed of my servant-girl!"[h]

In the penultimate episode of "Ein Landarzt" which follows, the doctor permits himself to be consecrated in his priestly calling. A choir of schoolchildren, directed by the village schoolteacher, sings an appropriately inappropriate hymn, since no one, it would seem, understands what the ceremony portends. Undressed by those assembled around him, the doctor finds himself being carried, stretched out, to the patient's bed, as if to an altar. He is placed next to the boy alongside the wound. Reconciled to his own fate of having been chosen to be one of the elect, the doctor must now reconcile his bedmate to his. He persuades him to accept the futility of his mission in life and to die peacefully. Appalled, perhaps, by this foreshadowing of his own demise, the doctor has yet another sudden and dramatic change of mind; he recants, refusing to accept the role in which the community has cast him. With the words "But now it was about time to think of saving myself" ("Aber jetzt war es Zeit, an meine Rettung zu denken"), he attempts to escape from the obligations which have just been ceremoniously heaped upon him. In thinking of his own rescue, he has completely forgotten Rosa. Since the word "rosa," meaning pink, has been placed at the head of the description of the wound, the implication is that it has supplanted the servant-girl and companion as a matter of supreme importance in the doctor's thinking. It is therefore now service in the cause of the wound, the carrying out of a mission not unlike that of Parzival, which the protagonist in "Ein Landarzt" now seeks to evade.

With the presupposition that the patient has died ("he became peaceful"/"er wurde still"), the narrative returns to the tense form with which it began — the past. The doctor struggles to reach the realm of reality out of which the horses had transported him, but fails, hurled on horseback into the region of limbo. It is the dimension of the eternal: "Never will I get back home" ("Niemals komme ich nach Hause"), the doctor laments. At the same time he has a vision of the future: "My flourishing practice is gone; a successor steals my fees" ("Meine blühende Praxis ist verloren; ein Nachfolger bestiehlt mich"). The climactic sentence in the story uses the tense form of the eternal present: "Naked, exposed to the frost of this most unhappy of times, I, an aged man, wander about."[i] As his voice (very like King Lear's) echoes out, he proclaims that he has been tricked into assuming a responsibility beyond his capacity to bear. The truth of his state in life, a representation of the actual dilemma which Kafka faced, becomes clear to the doctor. Recognizing his own inability to be in command of the horses, language in its imaginative dimension, and at the same time to divest himself of his need to set out on a futile quest (not unlike Don Quixote), the protagonist in "Ein Landarzt" is left with the knowledge that he is doomed to live in uncertainty. In the light of the title given a recent study of Kafka and his work, *Franz Kafka: Representative Man*,[7] the thesis of the story proposes that human beings confront a conflict which cannot be resolved; they live in two opposing worlds, one that is outside of them and one that is in them. Thus, like the doctor, they find themselves in limbo.

Although Kafka gave "Ein Landarzt" at least a nod of approval, his critics have, by and large, been less than enthusiastic. The blatant flaw discovered by many interpreters of the work lies, from their perspective, in its lack of structure; in this regard Hans P. Guth, an early commentator, contends: "Kafka's much analyzed 'Country Doctor' has

---

[7] Frederick R. Karl, *Franz Kafka: Representative Man* (New York: Ticknor & Fields, 1991).

the alogical surface texture of a dream...."[8] Kafka's abiding interest in his dreams cannot be dismissed, and they have no doubt left their imprint on his narratives. However, Kafka was plainly too conscientious an artist, a writer of fiction, to have been satisfied with a clinical report or a mere transcription of a dream in place of a story. In the same frame of reference, it is clear that the subtlety and consistency which prevails in Kafka's use of dreamlike symbols marks his devotion to the writing of fiction as an endeavor to acquire self-knowledge and through it to come to terms with a conflict-ridden existence. The importance of "Ein Landarzt" in the Kafka canon has been pointed out by Walter Sokel, who finds the symbol of the patient with the wound to be central in Kafka's portraiture of the artist. Specifically, Sokel identifies the sick youngster as the doctor's and therefore also Kafka's true self, "the pure 'I'" ("das reine Ich"), namely, the objective of his quest, his search for his life's import.

The last story in the *Ein Landarzt* collection, "Ein Bericht für eine Akademie" ("A Report for an Academy"), reiterates the thesis of the country doctor's story in a much more pellucid format. The didacticism of the animal fable, which Kafka tended to favor in choosing literary models, prevails in this tale of a humanized ape. Nevertheless, the relationship between the two narratives is a close one; the nexus which ties them together is the metaphor of the wound. The ape acquires two injuries when his about-to-be captors ambush and shoot him. One bullet scrapes his cheek, leaving a wound similar to the one which the groom inflicts on Rosa when he bites her on the cheek. This leaves a red scar which even provides the ape with a quasi-human name Rotpeter. A subtle reference to the failure of Kafka's attempt to keep Felice Bauer as a bride and muse may be found in this instance of convoluted symbolism. The second bullet inflicts a more serious injury on the animal as he seeks to escape capture; he is struck below the waist so that the wound lies in the same region as that of the patient in "Ein Landarzt." The suggestion that the injury in both cases results in impotence of a general as well as a sexual kind lies close at hand. When the wounded ape regains consciousness, he finds himself imprisoned in a narrow and low cage and realizes he seems doomed to die either in his cell or in any attempt to escape from it. The sound of his lamentation, so he is subsequently told, had convinced his captors that he was capable of being trained, and they had waited for him to recover. As he recalls his thought processes at the time, occurring in the manner of apes in the stomach, Rotpeter concludes that he had decried to himself mostly his lack of freedom, or more

[8] Hans P. Guth, "Symbol and Contextual Restraint," *PMLA*, 80:4/1 (Sept. 1965), 427.

aptly put, his lack of a way out (*Ausweg*, which, as Roy Pascal has pointed out, means "evasion" as well).[9] Like the doctor held captive in the regions of limbo, the ape is held in the vise of being unable to choose between liberation through death (letting the wound bring about his demise) or living while enduring enslavement. Since Rotpeter intuitively or in a kind of gut reaction distrusts the freedom envisioned as the result of risking his life, he makes the logical and realistic choice of staying alive. In turn, he is rewarded by being presented with the opportunity to select a way out, either life as an ape, but an imprisoned one, in Hagenbeck's zoo or life as an artiste (*not* artist) on the vaudeville stage. In effect the story ends with the protagonist's choice to become an entertainer, to turn his back on his true calling, in the service of which he had been anointed by his wounding. However, most interpreters have, quite appropriately, taken the remaining half of the narration into consideration and focussed their attention on the process of humanizing the ape undergoes. Learning to spit, to smoke, to become intoxicated, and to expose himself, which Rotpeter equates with learning to speak, to read, to write, and to reason, represents to most interpreters a critique on Kafka's part of humanity's claim to a God-given superiority over the so-called natural world. If "Ein Bericht für eine Akademie" were simply an animal fable with a moral (e.g., let human beings learn to be humble), it would not be a significant work in the Kafka canon. Its importance lies in its relationship to "Ein Landarzt," which it parodies, and to "Ein Hungerkünstler," which it presages. Frederick R. Karl in his biography/critique of Kafka emphasizes (and perhaps even overemphasizes) this aspect of the story: "'A Report (or Statement, Advice) to an Academy'... is central to Kafka's thinking."[10] The title itself provides a valuable clue to the narrative's many facets of meaning. It claims in labeling itself a report that it is not fiction but an account of a scientific experiment conducted with all objectivity. Gerhard Neumann has even suggested that the report is in reality a speech (*Antrittsrede*) delivered by the ape on the occasion of his installation as a member of the academy.[11] In a sense then, by providing this title, Kafka announces his intention to mock the kind of truth which results when it is based strictly on facts, on its referentiality. Rotpeter himself makes the point that in pulling down his trousers in order to exhibit his wound he is indeed merely

[9] Roy Pascal, *Kafka's Narrators* (Cambridge: Cambridge University Press, 1982), p. 195.

[10] Karl, *Franz Kafka: Representative Man*, p. 557.

[11] Gerhard Neumann, "Die Arbeit im Alchimistengäßchen," in *Kafkabuch II*, ed. Hartmut Binder (Stuttgart: Alfred Kröner, 1979), p. 334.

establishing its reality. "When it comes to truth," he says, "every high-minded individual will cast off (even) the most fastidious of manners."[j] Although the ape's training does indicate that civilization is only a thin veneer over the brutality which perseveres in human nature, this truism can hardly be the principal theme in an autobiographical narrative which concerns the inner life and concepts such as freedom and artistic integrity.

The common thread which runs through "Ein Landarzt," "Ein Bericht für eine Akademie," and, subsequently, "Ein Hungerkünstler" is an exposition of Kafka's devotion to the craft of writing and the personal accountability he owes, now no longer to his father but to those for whom he writes. The country doctor quickly forgets his newfound interest in Rosa which the groom has awakened in him and later also his concern for the sick young man and his obsequious family. In their stead he welcomes the entire community who make him their priest and shaman. The doctor's work as a healer of the body is accordingly elevated to a mission in the field of the literary arts. Its objective is the promulgation of truth in the form of self-knowledge. In an entry in a notebook, dated November 30, 1917, Kafka explained in this light the relationship between religious faith and faith in a calling: "To have faith means: to free the immutable in oneself, or more accurately: to free oneself, or more accurately: to be immutable, or more accurately: to be."[12k] In "Ein Landarzt" the protagonist does not believe in himself completely and is left stranded in the nowhere of his insecurity. The image of the half-man, half-ape symbolizes and satirizes Rotpeter's quandary, his lack of conviction and faith. He is the prime and most ridiculous example of one who has chosen to live securely in an unexplored state of mind rather than to live to die in a state of grace. In depicting the hunger-artist, Kafka created the ape's counterpart, the devout artist, and used the vehicle of fiction to write a hagiography. In that story the protagonist attempts to carry out his mission, to fulfill his obligation to the community, letting his art inform them about their own lives.

---

[12] Franz Kafka, *Hochzeitsvorbereitungen auf dem Lande* (Frankfurt am Main: Fischer, 1976), p. 66.

Notes

a. "Man weiß nicht was für Dinge man im eigenen Hause vorrätig hat" (112).

b. "Ich bin kein Weltverbesserer.... Ich bin vom Bezirk angestellt und tue meine Pflicht bis zum Rand, bis dorthin, wo es fast zu viel wird" (114).

c. "Noch für Rosa muß ich sorgen, dann mag der Junge recht haben und auch ich will sterben" (114).

d. "Rezepte schreiben ist leicht, aber im übrigen sich mit den Leuten verständigen, ist schwer" (114).

e. "Wer die Schönheit angeschaut mit Augen,/ Ist dem Tode schon anheimgegeben."

f. "Im spitzen Winkel mit zwei Hieben der Hacke geschaffen. Viele bieten ihre Seite an und hören kaum die Hacke im Forst, geschweige denn, daß sie ihnen näher kommt" (116).

g. "So sind die Leute in meiner Gegend, immer das Unmögliche vom Arzt verlangend" (115).

h. "Nun, wie es beliebt: ich habe mich nicht angeboten; verbraucht ihr mich zu heiligen Zwecken, lasse ich auch das mit mir geschehen; was will ich Besseres, alter Landarzt, meines Dienstmädchens beraubt!" (115).

i. "Nackt, dem Froste dieses unglückseligsten Zeitalters ausgesetzt, mit irdischen Wagen, unirdischen Pferden, treibe ich alter Mann mich umher" (117).

j. "Kommt es auf Wahrheit an, wirft jeder Großgesinnte die allerfeinsten Manieren ab" (140).

k. "Glauben heißt: das Unzerstörbare in sich befreien, oder richtiger: sich befreien, oder richtiger: unzerstörbar sein, oder richtiger: sein."

2

The Making of a Martyr

"EIN HUNGERKÜNSTLER" IS the title story and one of four which Kafka collected and arranged for publication in the last year of his life (1924); their interrelationship and its pertinence to the theme of the artist's dedication announced in the title cannot be disregarded. In this respect the first narrative in the book serves as an introductory exposition of the artist's identity and the purport of his life. Its title "Erstes Leid" ("First Sorrow" or perhaps "Early Sorrow") and the protagonist's occupation — rather than profession, that of a performer in a circus, a trapeze artist, indicate all too clearly that Kafka is continuing his portraiture of the writer with consistency in style and point of view. The same unique combination of realism and fantasy which character-ized the opening pages of "Die Verwandlung" prevails throughout the story of the acrobat on the trapeze. The swing dangerously high up above the arena's floor is not only the place where he performs his spectacular feats, it is also his home, his place of abode. Kafka carefully depicts the means by which the athlete is enabled to stay aloft and yet take care of his physical needs. At the same time, the bizarre nature of his devotion to his art immediately brings into focus the story's symbolic substance. In this vein, the trapeze artist's manager or agent, called an impresario, likewise plays a double role. He is a necessary part of the fiction since he enables the trapeze artist to fulfill his wish to live confined in the smallest of spaces, even smaller than a cage; on another level of the story, he supplants the antagonist, who creates obstacles for Kafka's antihero, the host of father figures in *Amerika/Der Verschollene*, for instance. Here the only other actual character in the very brief narrative does not impede the protagonist but overwhelms him with his concern. At one point his generosity, his willingness to provide the acrobat with an additional trapeze, causes his client to break into tears. The manager seems to me to represent Kafka's conviction that even the most improbable situation, the most fantastic, in which all hindrances are set aside and the conditions for achieving his goal (literally, the protagonist's) are met in every way, must still prove to be fruitless.

The trapeze artist's desire to put himself above the world and away from human contact, except for that with the indispensable impresario and a few brief visits from a fellow artist, springs from his recognition that he lives only for his art. The goal toward which he strives in his self-imposed isolation is perfection in his artistry; to that end he requires his manager to the let him double the difficulties involved in his feat. The paradoxical nature of the gymnast's lonely struggle lies in the fact that he performs precisely for the enlightenment of those from whom he has so infinitely far removed himself. He is in a double bind; in order to express to the degree of complete faultlessness his knowledge of what constitutes human destiny, he must himself experience a radically different kind of destiny. The impartial narrator reports that the trapeze artist is disturbed by meeting the occasional glance of someone in the audience; furthermore, he remains unaware even of those who come by and watch him admiringly in his moments of practice or rest. Heinz Hillmann has analyzed the artist's dilemma in these terms: "Therewith the fundamental question of humankind about the nature of their existence stays inexorably before him."[1a] Under these circumstances the writer's anguish is unavoidable, and his quandary remains without a solution. According to its title, "Erstes Leid" depicts the immediacy of Kafka's recognition of the incompatibility between living and writing; it occurred at the inception of his literary career. Writing to his first true friend Oskar Pollak, he expressed his despair at the thought of becoming an author: "God doesn't want me to write, but I — I must."[2b] The reference to the suffering of a young protagonist suggests a kinship with Goethe's portrait of his youthful self in *Die Leiden des jungen Werthers* (*The Sorrows of Young Werther*); it is noteworthy that Kafka read this most successful of Goethe's early works at the same time when he was writing "Beschreibung eines Kampfes" ("Description of a Struggle") in 1904. In 1913, on the point of involving himself in the composition of a second novel, *Der Prozeß* (*The Trial* or, more accurately, *The Hearing*), Kafka reread Goethe's story about an incipient artist living as an outcast.[3] Thus, "Erstes Leid" presents a portrait of the artist as a young man at the beginning of his mission, when he is only half-aware that it is fated to end unaccomplished.

---

[1] Heinz Hillmann, *Franz Kafka: Dichtungstheorie und Dichtungsgestalt* (Bonn: Bouvier/Herbert Grundmann, 1973), p. 73.

[2] Franz Kafka, *Briefe (1902-1924)* (New York: Schocken, 1958), p. 21.

[3] See "Kafka's Principal Works and His Recorded Private Reading" in *Twentieth Century Interpretations of "The Trial"*, ed. James Rolleston (Englewood Cliffs, N.J.: Prentice-Hall, 1976) — a chart without pagination.

The wrinkles which the impresario sees beginning to appear on the acrobat's smooth forehead presage the coming of the wound; as yet the artist himself has only a vague sense of his destiny. The tears he sheds in anticipation of his martyrdom place him in the company of others among Kafka's characters whose role it is to depict the dedicated artist-writer (such as Kafka conceived himself to be) at a point in his career before he has fully realized the tragic nature of his lot. The trapeze artist's tears are a sign more of his inability to abandon his quest than of his growing awareness of its futility. A predecessor to the protagonist in "Erstes Leid" is unmistakably another circus performer appearing in "Auf der Galerie" in *Ein Landarzt*; in this instance the acrobat is a girl, almost still a child, who balances herself on the back of a horse moving in a circle. This image imposes itself, as Brentano's terminology would have it, on the consciousness of a visitor to the circus, watching from a seat up in the gallery. The impartial narrator describes the brief episode of a (figurative) confrontation between the two characters in two paragraphs, one of which contains principally subjunctive verb forms while the other uses a plethora of verbs in the present indicative. In effect, this arrangement produces two versions of the same scene, one as the viewer in the gallery perceives it and one as it exists in reality, in its referentially verifiable aspect. However, it is clear from the conclusion of the story — it has the nature of a parable — that the visitor's perception also expresses truth, if of a different kind, the intuitive kind. If the young man in the gallery is taken to represent the writer as Kafka envisions him, then his knowledge of the little bareback rider's life may be just as accurate as knowledge based on so-called facts; it would certainly be less superficial.[4] Mindful of the fact that his version of reality will never come to prevail over the version accepted as truth by most of humanity, the young man in the gallery seat lowers his head and begins to cry helplessly. The image suggests that of the author, removed from the everyday world, looking down on life from his vantage point on high, sensing but not allowing himself to acknowledge the futility of his endeavors.

The same figure appears in another, even briefer narrative in *Ein Landarzt*, titled "Eine kaiserliche Botschaft" ("A Message from the Emperor"). Kafka excised the passage from a longer work "Beim Bau der Chinesischen Mauer" ("Concerning the Construction of the Great

---

[4] In his article "Logic and Ontology in Kafka's Fiction," Arnold Heidsieck posits: "Eternal reality comes to consciousness as seemingly phenomenal (intentional) reality and knowledge about it must therefore remain uncertain." See *The Dove and the Mole*, ed. Moshe Lazar & Ronald Gottesman (Malibu: Undena Publications, 1987), p. 200.

Wall of China"), which he never prepared for publication.[5] The remoteness of the observer at the circus from the world he describes reappears, greatly magnified, as a motif in this tersely told anecdote. The narrator, who may or may not shed his anonymity and impartiality in the episode's last sentence, pictures a country as vast as a continent (China), in which the symbol of absolute authority, the source of truth, the emperor dwells, together with his court, in a region inaccessible to his subjects. Yet it is the obligation of the emperor to share his wisdom or knowledge with everyone, even the most insignificant of his underlings; to that end he has appointed a messenger to bring the benefaction of his words to all. Since the emperor is dying, that is to say, the possibility that absolute values exist is becoming more and more remote, he can only whisper his message to his courier and must ask to have him repeat it. The narrator confides: "The message was so important to him that he had it repeated in his ear" (128).[c] At this point the messenger becomes the principal figure in the narrative. That Kafka intends him to stand for the writer cannot be too farfetched a supposition; patently he is called to deliver a message from a nearly abstract source to all manner of people. Like the circus acrobat or, for that matter, the man from the country seeking admittance to the law, he is indefatigable in his efforts to complete his task. (There is some direct similarity between "Vor dem Gesetz" and "Eine kaiserliche Botschaft" in that, in the first instance, the doorkeeper bends down to hear the dying man's last words, while in the latter, the messenger bends down to hear the emperor; yet the implication of the action in the one case is the reverse of that in the other.) Despite the devotion of the emperor's ambassador in carrying out his duties, he cannot overcome the impediments which bar his way. Just passing beyond the bounds of the emperor's estate seems an impossibility; this barrier suggests on the symbolic level the difficulties involved in finding words to express what is largely ineffable. Any progress beyond that point that the messenger might make is stated in terms of the unreal with subjunctive, contrary-to-fact verb forms. Further hindrances are placed in his path through the mundane world; the very first of the intended recipients of the information he brings could not be reached in millennia. While the emperor's agent and the impossible feat he undertakes have held the

---

[5] *Ein Landarzt* contains yet another example of a narrative excised from a larger work, in this instance *Der Prozeß*. This excerpt, "Vor dem Gesetz" ("Before the Law"), the significance of which critics are apt to concede, provides if not a key to the novel at least important information in regard to its meaning and the meaning of Kafka's work in general. The excision of "Eine kaiserliche Botschaft" can also be assumed to have served an equally significant purpose.

narrator's full attention in the story's central section, another figure appears and becomes prominent in the last sentence of "Eine kaiserliche Botschaft," a kind of epilogue. It reads: "You, however, are seated at your window and let the message come through in your dreaming, when the evening comes" (129).[d] The "you," specifically "thou," is vastly ambiguous; it might indicate that the narrator has dropped his impersonal stance and made an appearance, by addressing himself, in this third-person, objectively told anecdote. The import of such an intrusion would be that he (or she), the writer, could intuitively accomplish what all the toil of a realistically inclined author would fail to accomplish. Providing such a denouement would be strikingly uncharacteristic of Kafka, especially in view of the negativity present in his other narratives of this kind. An interpretation of this scene which gives the story a less exceptional outcome takes the person identified as "you" to be Kafka himself rather than his amanuensis; under these circumstances Kafka can express more directly the melancholy of his situation by proposing that he can only bring his mission to a successful conclusion in a dream. This reading of the end of "Eine kaiserliche Botschaft" appears to have some validity in the light of (yet) another but lengthier narrative also from the *Ein Landarzt* collection, which Kafka similarly published by itself, removed from a larger context — "Ein Traum," originally a part of *Der Prozeß*. The story describes a dream the novel's protagonist Josef K. has; in it he confronts in a cemetery an artist imprinting a tombstone. Kafka says of this protagonist: "K. was inconsolable over the artist's state, he began to weep and sobbed for a long time into his cupped hands" (138).[e] Josef K. soon discovers that his name is being written on the grave marker and finds release from his sorrow while burrowing his way into his grave.

The futility of the effort these characters, the trapeze artist, the messenger, the man from the country, put into their endeavor to acquire and/or convey vital information is not clear to them; they do not despair and accept total defeat, but persevere. Kafka's aspiration to raise his fiction to the level of the pure, the true, the immutable continues to be the dominating force in his life. Shimon Sandbank has emphasized the audacity of Kafka's ambition as a writer; he concludes: "Were it not for the fact that the doctrine Kafka was after was the total meaning of experience, the total truth of ontology rather than the partial truths of psychology or ethics or politics, he could have had a doctrine, not only its 'relics.'"[6]

---

[6] Shimon Sandbank, *After Kafka* (Athens: University of Georgia Press, 1989), p. 4.

The theme of encountering impediments on his way to reaching the pinnacle of literary accomplishment dominates Kafka's rather subdued narrative "Eine kleine Frau" ("A Little Woman"), the second of the *Ein Hungerkünstler* stories. In it, the narrator identifies himself only as an "I" who exists to the extent that he confronts the disapproval of a little woman, otherwise unknown to him, and the disinterest of the public. Although Dora Diamant (Dymant), Kafka's companion and care-giver in the last months of his life, has proposed that the protagonist's nemesis in the story was actually the woman from whom Kafka rented their first housing in Berlin, it is probable that this touch of reality in the fiction represents (as does the first-person storyteller) another instance of his undergirding of the artistic truth with a thin layer of referentially established truth. The narrator pictures her to himself as unfailingly wearing the same clothes: "(Her gown) is made of a yellowish gray, to a degree wood-colored material and is embellished with tassels or button-like ornaments of the same color" (183).[f] Her apparent insistence upon always wearing the same costume implies, as it does in the case of other characters in Kafka's work, a certain inflexibility in her thinking. The reference to wood in the description of the woman's dress puts her in the same class with natural phenomena, and she becomes an object in the world external to the protagonist's consciousness, an object which, according to Brentano's philosophy, forces him to focus his attention on it.

It becomes apparent to the observer that, despite her peculiarity and individuality, the little woman comes from the normal or everyday world to which he is accountable. The dichotomous viewpoint of the artist — the protagonist's complete lack of identity allows all manner of assumptions — comes to light in the description of the woman's hand which the narrator provides. Combining imaginative insight with commonsense, he reports: "The impression which her hand makes on me I can only reproduce by saying that I have never yet seen a hand, each of whose fingers are so distinctly set off from the others as they are in her case; and yet her hand exhibits by no means any anatomical irregularity — it is a completely normal hand" (184).[g] This double vision results in the protagonist's falling gradually into a state of paranoia. Although he has absolutely no contact with the little, that is, unprepossessing woman, he considers her to be his judge. By observing her and changing the shape of her hand, he has threatened her selfhood. He indicts himself on the charge that he has assaulted her by making her a part of his fiction. In turn, the torment he has inflicted on her becomes his torment. In the light of the other three stories in *Ein Hungerkünstler*, "Eine kleine Frau" can also be seen as a commentary on the artist's relationship to his art, or

Kafka's relationship to his writing. The interaction between the author and his story is the first aspect of the situation which Kafka explores; the protagonist contends: "Also a certain responsibility rests on my shoulders, since no matter how much the little woman is a stranger to me, and since so very much the only connection which exists between us two is the anger which I ascribe to (literally, prepare for) her, or, rather, the anger which she allows me to inflict on her, I dare not let myself be indifferent as to how (much) she suffers visibly and indeed physically from this anger" (185).[h] The protagonist/narrator does not let a friend persuade him to avoid the suffering he shares with his in effect prosecutor/victim by going away; rather, he intensifies his discomfort by concluding that his little judge ("meine kleine Richterin") is hatching out a sinister plot. "Perhaps she even hopes that, if the public should once decide to direct all their attention to me, a general public rage will arise against me and with its great resources of power will pronounce an ultimate sentence on me more quickly and mightily than her, of course, relatively weaker private rage is capable of doing; but then she will retreat, take a deep breath, and turn her back on me" he proposes (185).[i] The state of affairs that the writer (the author of "Eine kleine Frau") describes to himself has the effect of making him acknowledge that he has a double burden to bear. (In the same vein the trapeze artist has recognized his need for a second trapeze.) On the one hand he must meet the requirements, the high standards, that he has set for himself in his writing — he must judge himself; the little woman symbolizes in this regard the pain of his own dissatisfaction with his work. Kafka's sense of attainment which he experienced with the completion of "Ein Landarzt" seems never to have returned. But now there is another area of discontent; the relationship between the author and his readers has become a matter of grave concern to him. He assumes that, if his work can intrude on the public's indifference, it can only raise their ire; they will be outraged by having the suffering caused by the import of his fiction imposed on them. Laden with a double yoke of concerns, the painful insufficiencies of the work he produces and the inadequate response it receives, the protagonist in "Eine kleine Frau" can take comfort only in the process of ageing which everyone and everything undergoes. The intensity of both perception and expectation diminish in time, even though the problem remains the same — insoluble.

Because of the placidly resigned tone of the story's conclusion and its mundane setting critics have tended to neglect it or to regard it as an anomaly in *Ein Hungerkünstler*. Roy Pascal places it among those late narratives he finds to be slighter in form and concerned with an obsession "more accidental, less malign, less mortal."[7] In other words, he considers the protagonist's paranoia to have no symbolic value. Contrarily, in his discussion of "Eine kleine Frau," Heinz Hillmann takes great pains to found its pertinence and significance. He concludes that the little woman represents to the narrator who is the quintessence of conventionality his anathema; she forces him to face his meaningless life. Hillmann maintains: "What it is that has entered into his life through the existence of the little woman, that which has opened up on his body *like a wound* he must hide, has become distressing in the course of time" (my italics).[8j] Thus the threat of the artist's being overwhelmed by the demand of a largely bourgeois society that he conform to its conventions becomes the protagonist's bête noire, supplanting to an extent the authoritative father figure in Kafka's fiction. (It lingered in his life as his undelivered letter to his father, published as "Brief an den Vater," testifies.) For Hillmann the little woman is a counterforce in the contention for the writer's sense of self and belief in his mission: "She appears as the absolute other, the inexplicable in the unindividualized world of mere advancement and respectability."[9k] Hillmann concludes his exposition of "Eine kleine Frau" with an expansion and revision of the concept of "man," anyone, the faceless majority. Since serving humanity by uplifting it is the writer/artist's mission, Hillmann proposes that the protagonist, the "I" in the story, must not remove himself completely from the everyday world and live in an isolation such as that of the trapeze artist. He must, in a sense, reach a compromise with the little woman and let the exclusivity of his devotion to art come to an end. This reading of the story has the advantage of pointing the way to other narratives which followed in Kafka's literary career, such as "Forschungen eines Hundes" and "Josefine," which take up the theme of the relevance of art to society. At the same time, the reversal of values in the symbolism, regarding the bad-to-good influence of the woman on the narrator, seems to me to be uncharacteristic of Kafka and out of place in a story which he used to probe matters of great concern to him.

Written at least in large part, if not entirely, in 1922,[10] "Forschun-

---

[7] Roy Pascal, *Kafka's Narrators* (Cambridge: Cambridge University Press, 1982), p. 188.

[8] Heinz Hillmann, *Franz Kafka: Dichtungstheorie und Dichtungsgestalt*, p. 75.

[9] Ibid., p. 77.

[10] Because of a reference to a "Hundegeschichte" (dog story) in Kafka's journal for the year 1916, some critics, Heinz Hillmann, for example, have assumed that he made a foiled effort to write "Forschungen" at that time. Although non-specific,

gen eines Hundes" ("Investigations — better, The Research — of a Dog") clearly concerns itself with the relationship between the artist and his art as well as his public. In contrast to "Eine kleine Frau," the events of which occur in the drab, mundane world, Kafka has chosen for the "Forschungen," almost necessarily, the form of the animal fable, one he favored on a number of occasions. In his fictitious menagerie there are an ape, a mole, a mouse, jackals, a horse, a giant beetle, at least two humans who take on the mannerisms of a dog, and more of that ilk. In accord with the import of this literary genre, the animals in the story represent not only human beings but also a particular human trait with which certain members of the animal kingdom have become associated; thereby the fox is sly, the mouse fearful, the horse proud and gallant. Kafka has elected to make his protagonist and narrator a dog in order to establish at the outset that he is nondescript and humble.

In this regard the title "Forschungen eines Hundes" is paradoxical; only properly educated human beings engage in research. In addition, the fact that the unidentified (even by name) dog has ventured, even dared to undertake a scientific project has special significance. His search will be one for a practical kind of truth, for information which will benefit all of dogdom. It is of note that Kafka himself began his literary career with a collection of pithy prose pieces titled *Betrachtung*, which has been vaguely translated as *Meditation(s)* instead of as, precisely, *Observation*. The verb "betrachten" implies a close examination and is scarcely a synonym for "nachdenken" (to meditate or ponder over). In a similar fashion the ape's story has been labeled a report. Indeed a number of Kafka's protagonists have occupations which call for scientific or special training: the doctor in "Ein Landarzt," the travelling salesman or company agent in "Die Verwandlung," the land surveyor in *Das Schloß*, the globe-trotting researcher in "In der Strafkolonie," the bank official in *Der Prozeß*; there are also a lawyer and several businessmen who appear in minor roles. In his fiction Kafka occupies himself with the confusion which results when the rationality of the everyday world is confronted and confounded by the eruption in this safe and sound milieu of the irregular, the baroque with its writhing forms. In "Forschungen eines Hundes," accordingly, the dog-narrator begins his autobiographical account with his description of his first encounter with the bizarre. In

---

Kafka's comments are not inappropriate with a view to the themes he developed in the story completed in 1922; he says of "Hundegeschichte": "It is awful and gives me a headache. In spite of all the truth (in it), it is bad, pedantic, mechanistic (like) a fish still living but short of breath (dying) on a sandbank." ("Es ist trotz aller Wahrheit böse, pedantisch, mechanisch auf einer Sandbank ein noch knapp atmender Fisch.")

the midst of his humdrum young manhood, characterized as "the ordinary, quiet, happy everyday life" ("das gewöhnliche, ruhige, glückliche Leben des Tages"), he caught sight of seven musical dogs.[11] Strangely enough, the word "musical" pertains to the effect their performance had on the observer rather than to the talent they displayed, which consisted of standing on their hind legs. The eccentricity of their raising themselves above the level of the commonplace so overwhelmed the down-to-earth dog that he began to hear unearthly music — "especially awesome or lofty music" ("besonders schreckliche oder erhabene Musik," BK 186). The dog could make no contact with the prancing canines, and they, together with the astral harmonies they evoked, soon disappeared like a mirage. This initial event (there are only two or three in the entire story) with its musical overtones resembles many such occasions in Kafka's work. In "Ein Landarzt," so the doctor reveals, the disruption in his life began with the ringing of his night-bell; the observer in the gallery seat at the circus not only sees the tormented bareback rider but also hears the music accompanying her act. Of equal significance is the singing or humming the "land surveyor" hears over the telephone line which almost makes contact with the castle. The appearance of the dancing dogs and the ethereal sounds he hears cause the protagonist in "Forschungen" to determine to examine his hitherto meaningless life and to research the means by which it is sustained — the source (food) which nourishes it.

Interpreters of the text have, of course, found it necessary to explain first of all the symbolism of the seven musical dogs; their explications range from the almost superficial to the most profound. In regard to the former, several commentators concur in identifying the unabashedly perverse dogs ("these dogs were violating the law" / "diese Hunde hier vergingen sich gegen das Gesetz," BK 185) as a troupe of trained dogs responding to musical cues. Reading "Forschungen" on this (literal) level, which approaches that of allegory, would, however, require giving the central feature of the story, the dog's research into the origin of the nourishment which sustains him and his kind, an equally simplistic interpretation. The commonsense and obvious explanation, which the narrator himself scrupulously avoids making, must be, as these critics have pointed out, that objects or other beings exist in the world who dispense the food. Perhaps the unkafkaesque message contained in a thus oriented animal fable would have to be:

---

[11] Franz Kafka, *Beschreibung eines Kampfes* (Frankfurt am Main: Fischer, 1976), p. 187. Further references will appear in the text itself with the rubric BK.

dogs, or in their stead people, should not ignore, no less bite, the hand that feeds them.

In contrast to this kind of explication proffered by quite knowledgeable, if not perspicacious readers who wish to emphasize the story's gentle irony and Kafka's playfulness in devising its imagery,[12] completely opposed conclusions have been drawn by commentators who are persuaded that the narrative as a whole constitutes the quintessence of Kafka's fiction. In his study of the work, Walter Sokel makes this summary statement: "The dog-story is of the greatest significance for an understanding of the symbol of the pure self (the 'I')."[13] In her essay "Das Spätwerk" in the *Kafka-Handbuch* Ingeborg Henel catalogues the range of abstruse topics covered in "Forschungen": "While Kafka in his other stories treats (only) a specific problem, he undertakes in *The Research* (an exposition of) the entire range of intellectual life: the truth, the problem of the scientific approach, the question of progress, the arts, and the significance of religion, of its cultic form (of expression) — dance and song, as well as its systematic formulation (the science of music)."[14] These views of a story written, at least mainly, in 1922 when Kafka was preoccupied with the personal and literary interests that underlie *Das Schloß* and stories such as "Ein Hungerkünstler" and "Der Bau" ("The Burrow" or, better, "The Structure") must be of greater relevance to an explication of the text than those that take "Forschungen" to be the result of an exercise in literary wit.

In the guise of an unprepossessing animal fable (in structure it resembles "Ein Bericht für eine Akademie," but in intent rises far above the earlier tale), Kafka has set out to provide a broad-based analysis of his purpose in writing, his obligation as an author to society, and the prospect for the achievement of his aims. The episode of the so-called musical dogs which occurs at the very beginning of the narrative in all probability relates to his authorship. It describes what must be his initiation into the service of art. Through exposure to the "otherness" of the outrageous dancing dogs, the protagonist (who is

---

[12] See Roy Pascal, *Kafka's Narrators*, p. 213: "The story does not offer a great message but remains tentative and retains its humorous self-depreciating character to the end." See also Ritchie Robertson, *Kafka: Judaism, Politics, and Literature* (Oxford: Clarendon Press, 1985), p. 279: "Since the dominant tone of *Forschungen* is satirical, however, attempts to extract recondite messages from it risk being heavy-handed."

[13] Walter H. Sokel, *Franz Kafka: Tragik und Ironie* (Munich/Vienna: Albert Langen/Georg Müller, 1964), p. 209.

[14] Ingeborg Henel, "Das Spätwerk," *Kafka Handbuch II*, p. 237 f.

also the narrator) is forced to confront his own deficiencies. The situation, as he sees it, produces both the contrast between "great masters" ("große Meister") and a society of underlings and the sudden insight he has acquired in their presence, which creates a bond between them and himself: "as if I were one of the musicians myself," he reports, "although I was really only their victim," (that is, as a martyr for them).[n] Pointedly, Kafka makes music, i.e., the aesthetic sphere, here and throughout the fable, the key factor in the symbolism. Although amusical himself, Kafka seems to have been in accord with many German authors who have expressed their dissatisfaction with the imprecision of words and their envy of composers for the direct effect their music achieves. Some commentators hold, together with the narrator, that this "especially awesome or noble music" ("besonders schreckliche oder erhabene Music") must have a supernatural source; the dog writes, once again using the subjunctive, that what he had heard had been ethereal sounds — "as if nature itself might be a miscalculation" ("als sei die Natur ein Fehler," BK 185). This half-per-ceived manifestation of the immaterial in the material realm (already pictured in "Ein Landarzt" by the sudden appearance and subsequent neighing of the horses) constitutes a call to the researcher to become one of the elect, the artists, who convey to mortals intimations of the immortal. (In *The Glass Bead Game* or *Das Glasperlenspiel*, Hermann Hesse joins living and dead artists together in the community of the immortals.) Kafka's dog researcher, starting out on his quest to discover the source of that which sustains life, first establishes that the kind of knowledge he strives to obtain is different from the kind to be found through scientific investigation — which he calls "true science" ("die wahre Wissenschaft"), probably to contrast it with "the science of truth" ("die Wissenschaft des Wahren"). He disclaims having the ability to make use of scientific research. "It wouldn't occur to me to get mixed up with true science; I have all due respect for it, but to contribute to it, I (just) lack the knowledge and industry and peace of mind and, not lastly, especially for some years now, the inclination."[o]

Ironically, the dog immediately proceeds to carry out various enervating, even life-threatening experiments to establish what is intrinsically knowable or true. This category of "inner" truth has been relegated by scientists and philosophers to the realm of art and called artistic, that is, aesthetic truth and/or implied truth.[15] Kafka's dog

[15] See Käte Hamburger, *Wahrheit und ästhetische Wahrheit* (Stuttgart: Klett-Cotta, 1979). John Hospers defines "implied" truth in this way: "The novel does not *state* truths about human nature; but it presents them indirectly by simply *being* true-to (sic) human nature...," John Hospers, *Meaning and Truth in the Arts* (Chapel Hill: University of North Carolina Press, 1946), p. 205.

seeks to find the *source* of this ultimate truth, made manifest in the fable by the symbol of food, that which enables him and his kind to exist. "All knowledge," he contends, "the totality of all questions and all answers, is contained within dogs."P At this point he begins his martyrdom, starving himself in order to compel the dispenser of this vital nourishment to reveal itself. He knows that, in accord with the traditional explanation, food simply erupts from the earth, but decides to challenge this much too superficial an answer to a dilemma by refusing to eat what appears before him on the ground. Subsequently, he does, on occasion, find that sustenance will descend on or round about him. The thought seems to elude him that nourishment might be an inner process. To alleviate his confusion, he then hides himself, believing that the force providing the food will have to seek him out. It doesn't, and he starves himself almost to death. This episode in "Forschungen" has to a great degree the intensity of the intellectual struggle between God and Job; however, in the biblical account it is God who challenges Job rather than the reverse, which is clearly the case in Kafka's narrative. John Winkelmann has provided a reading of the text based on the premise that the dog is searching for religious truth. He proposes: "The dog's quest for the meaning of existence is the eternally hopeless human quest, which in the case of human beings could attain its object only if God would make himself manifest to the senses.[16] Thereby, the encounter with the seven dogs standing on their hind legs becomes a visit from a host of angels, the existence of the unchewable bone containing "the noblest marrow" ("das edelste Mark") the equivalent of the Holy Grail, and the appearance of a princely hunting dog a vision of the redeemer. Although this interpretation has the aura of plausibility that sometimes accompanies Janouch's renderings of his conversations with Kafka, it likewise falls short of being truly relevant to Kafka's principal concerns.[17] The obviously autobiographical frame of reference in which Kafka's fiction is set is disregarded in a reading which holds "Forschungen" to have basically a religious connotation. The search for truth which emerges from an exploration of the self, of consciousness, namely an inner truth, would suggest itself, therefore, as a more secure foundation on which to rest the by no means obvious symbolism in the narrative. In

[16] John Winkelmann, "Kafka's 'Forschungen eines Hundes,'" *Monatshefte*, 59:3 (Fall 1967), 207.

[17] In a footnote Winkelmann almost gives an alternative reading: "Since music stands for *art* in general as a mysterious link to the divine, it might be thought that the 'Wissenschaft der Musik' could equally well stand for esthetics. However, in the total it evidently stands for theology," ibid., 215n.

that light commentators have interpreted the performing dogs as representing the small troupe of East European Jewish actors who brought the Yiddish theater to Prague for a brief stay.[18] At that time as a beginning and "part-time" writer, Kafka struggled not only with self-doubt about pursuing his avocation and his father's scornful disapproval of it but also with his fear of becoming completely isolated by way of his literary endeavors. In the story the protagonist laments: "I was left completely on my own" ("ich war völlig auf mich allein angewiesen," BK 193). The insight that Kafka attained as a result of his association with the visiting actors produced recognition on Kafka's part of the capacity of art to involve and improve the lot of social groups by providing them with self-knowledge, enabling them to play their role as individuals and members of the community. Thus for the researcher the seven "musical" dogs embody, as he knows intuitively, the possibility of a symbiotic relationship between the artist and society; they have caused him to question himself and his kind and to try to find the key to the meaning of existence itself.

A symbol which occurs subsequently in the story related to that of the dancing dogs is the phenomenon (or chimera) publicized in the "folk"-lore of the canine world of the "Lufthunde" ("dogs poised in air" or, inaccurately, "soaring dogs"). With the aerial dogs Kafka can but be parodying the symbol of the musical dogs and all it entails. These self-levitating dogs — boldly and perhaps, once more, ironically Kafka proposes that they might have been called artists (BK 195) — produce little, if any work; their function is to hover in air as a conductor of phantom vibrations from above. They are empty vessels, so the dog engaged in his heroic experiments contends, containing only echoes of ultimate truth. He sums up their achievement in this way: "And therewith will appear, if indeed not the truth — never will one come so far or reach that height — but, rather, something like the deep confusion of lying or untruthfulness."[q] They can raise themselves only briefly above the commonplace; they, too are bound to the earth.

Not inconsequently, before deciding to end his fruitless quest to ascend to the source of existential (ontological) truth, the researcher fixes his attention on the ground, where the food involved in his study usually lies waiting; that is, he concentrates on the material aspect of his investigation of the abstract. He finds an image which will depict this form of nourishment at least to his own satisfaction; it is that of a bone encased in a shatter-proof shell, containing "the noblest marrow"

---

[18] See, for example, Walter A. Strauss, *On the Threshold of a New Kabbalah* (New York, etc.: Peter Lang, 1988), p. 159.

("das edelste Mark") — the self-knowledge which is the earthly form of "the true" ("das Wahre"). Yet even this earthly manna is unobtainable; not one of all dog-kind has teeth strong enough to split the bone open. However, so the protagonist in "Forschungen" puts forth, if all canine jaws were to clamp down simultaneously on it, they would crush the shell. Underlining the irony implicit in the achievement of this impossible exploit with a paradox, the dog insists that such a community effort would actually be unnecessary, since the mere resolution of all, artist and non-artist alike, to act in concert would cause a spontaneous splitting of the bone. Self-knowledge would pour out, obviating the need for sheer truth to come spiraling down from above. In his book on Kafka's work, Wilhelm Emrich takes "the noblest marrow" to be "a completely valid knowledge of 'truth' which (simply) is in all dogs."[19] Unable, like the prancing dogs and the aerial dogs, to snatch the truth, enlightenment or ultimate knowledge about human existence, out of the air and despairing of being able to convey the significance of his experiments, or his writing, to his contemporaries, the researcher gives up his fast, the attempt to evoke the presence of an all-embracing intelligence.[20] He has reached the nadir of his belief in the effectiveness of his work. Part of the blame for his failure he assigns to the community of dogs. To himself he represents society as asking rather cynically: "Hadn't I wanted this isolation (for myself)?" and then responds to himself: "Indeed (I did), you dogs, but not so as to end (die) here, but rather to cross over into truth out of this world of lies, where there is no one from whom one can learn the truth, even not from me, native citizen of (the land) of lies (that I am)."[T]

The frustrated dog is rescued from the pit into which he has fallen by the sudden appearance — in its nature it resembles the vision of the performing dogs — of a self-assured hunting dog who looks down at him and commands him to arise. This penultimate symbol in "Forschungen" would in all probability have, because of the intensely personal tone of the story, autobiographical significance. At this point in his life, Kafka had established a close relationship with Robert Klopstock, whose bout with tuberculosis had interrupted the pursuit of a career in medicine. As a fellow patient with a capacity to appreciate, although from an outsider's viewpoint, Kafka's literary aspirations and the hopelessness he felt of his ever achieving their

[19] Wilhelm Emrich, *Franz Kafka* (Frankfurt am Main: Athenäum, 1960, II. Auflage), p. 52; the quotation reads: "ein vollgültiges Wissen um die 'Wahrheit', die in allen Hunden 'ist.'"

[20] Emrich calls this kind of truth "a total overview" ("der totale Überblick").

realization, Klopstock served for Kafka as an element in society sympathetic to his concept of the writer's role and sensitive to his susceptibility to feelings of isolation and failure. The hunting dog's challenge to the researcher to resume his quest, expressed in the narrative by the protagonist's perception that he is singing, arouses the forlorn canine instantly: "But I was already in flight, sent aloft by the melody, in (a series of) the most glorious leaps."[s] The emotionalism of the encounter between the two characters has suggested to Emrich that the bond linking them and thus figuratively the artist and society has been forged by love, that is, the love of one human being for another. "The importuning dog is one who loves," Emrich contends.[21] He concludes that the protagonist now realizes that an intellectual quest needs to be undergirded by an ardent commitment to act on behalf of others. On the autobiographical level, this episode in "Forschungen," I would propose, gives expression to Kafka's need to justify through a conclusive statement his writing and/or his compulsion to write. At first he had sought to explain his sense of mission to himself and a few friends, then at a crucial moment to his family, especially to his father (to whom he dedicated the *Landarzt* collection); lastly, when doomed by his "wound," tuberculosis, he sought to address all those for whose enlightenment he had worn himself sore by his writing — an enlightenment he himself had but glimpsed.

Kafka ended (it must be presumed) his story of the canine researcher by presenting him as working on yet another, and perhaps his last project, the development of "the theory of the song which calls for nourishment to descend" ("die Lehre von dem die Nahrung herabrufenden Gesang"). Pointedly, Kafka's protagonist finds that, in the final analysis, the role of the creative artist in society is that of a teacher-guide to humanity. The proposition that art, here "song," can and concurrently should serve as a source of intellectual sustenance which encourages the growth of self-knowledge implies that Kafka had reconciled himself to the impossibility of arriving at an ultimate or absolute form of knowledge in his fiction.[22] He had become convinced, moreover, that self-knowledge had as its consequence freedom for the individual, whereas living in ignorance would constitute imprisonment in a network of lies. The kind of relationship between

[21] Emrich, *Franz Kafka*, p. 162; the quotation reads: "Der drohende Hund ist ein Liebender."

[22] See Allen Thiher, *Franz Kafka: A Study of the Short Fiction* (Boston: Twayne, 1990), p. 7: "A text's function is to communicate a message or perhaps some form of knowledge over a distance from some sending source to some receiving source."

the artist and society that would cast the former in the role of a purveyor of inner truths has been labeled inadequate by at least one of the most knowledgeable of the critics of Kafka's work. In his book *Kafka's Narrators*, Roy Pascal has found him wanting as a preceptor. "The lack of a moral-social dimension," Pascal writes, "is a feature that in my view seriously diminishes the stature of Kafka in the perspective of the world's great literature."[23] Both the fable and the parable, narrative forms employed frequently by Kafka, lend themselves to use as a means of direct communication between the writer/artist and society. The story of "Forschungen" reveals its author and narrator to have been an outsider, intent upon accomplishing an impossible feat, the uncovering of the source of all knowledge, of finding the root of selfhood; eventually, having defined his role as that of a guide, he has become a humble member of his kind, paradoxically, such as he was at the beginning of his investigations. In 1917, about when he may first have tried to write a "dog-story," Kafka also undertook the task of defining the concept of truth in an entry in one (the fourth) of his notebooks. He proclaimed: "There exist for us two kinds of truth, just as depicted by the tree of knowledge and the tree of life. The truth of the doer(s) and the truth of the quiescent. In the first (case) good separates itself from evil, in the second there is nothing but the good itself, and it (the good) can comprehend neither good nor evil. The first truth we have in reality, the second only intuitively. That is the sad state of affairs. The happy one is that the first (kind of) truth belongs but to the moment, the second (kind of truth) to eternity; therefore the first kind of truth will also be expunged in the light of the second."[24t] It can readily be inferred that Kafka was describing, first, truth which can be referentially established and then truth which is only perceived intuitively. Accordingly, the "food" concerning which the dog in "Forschungen" does his research can be of two kinds. Lying on the ground, it has a physical presence and a practical purpose, enabling the individual, in the interests of surviving, to judge between that which is good and that which is evil. But, as the dog discovers through his encounter with the artistic dogs and through his attempts to understand the myth of the ethereal dogs, there is an intangible and inedible food (as such it is similar to music) which nourishes the

---

[23] Pascal, *Kafka's Narrators*, p. 215. Nevertheless, Pascal values the power of Kafka's prose: "So Kafka's dog reveals even in baseless speculations about musical dogs or 'air dogs' a power of imagination and logic beyond that of his community" (p. 215 f.).

[24] Franz Kafka, *Hochzeitsvorbereitungen auf dem Lande* (Frankfurt am Main: Fischer, 1976), p. 80.

individual as well as provides for his survival. The researcher finds that his experiments, so costly in regard to his health, in trying to provide his "fellow" dogs with information about moral values, have been largely unsuccessful. However, instead of despairing, he turns to the more difficult, if not impossible task of researching the nature and source of true knowledge or knowledge about the truth — "the science of music" ("die Wissenschaft der Musik"). The theme of the two kinds of food or the very nature of food becomes the center of Kafka's attention in "Ein Hungerkünstler" ("A Hunger Artist"), but there the hopeful conclusion he reaches in the animal fable (implicit in the form) is replaced by a dirge and tragedy.[25]

The philosophical sketch on the subject of the tree of knowledge and the tree of life has a connection, if a slight and tenuous one, with Kafka's description of the three values with which he strives to endow his fiction. Obviously, one of his goals is the representation of the truth, "das Wahre." It is the centerpiece in Kafka's triptych. In positioning the elements in his triad of attributes, however, Kafka puts "the pure," out of the realm of human morality, first. In this way he pays heed to the conflict between good (the pure) and evil (the impure) which prevails in earthly life. Simultaneously, the pure signifies the perfect, the beautiful, in art. The immutable ("das Unveränderliche") with which Kafka ended the series expressing his literary aspirations, pertains, in consequence, to the province of the arts which is projected into the dimension of the eternal. As the central element, truth is a component of the other two, as the dog-researcher perceives and informs the (disinterested) dog community.

---

[25] See Robertson, *Kafka: Judaism, Politics, and Literature*, p. 276: "If *Das Schloß* is a tragedy, then *Forschungen eines Hundes* corresponds to the satyr-play that rounded off the Greek tragic cycles."

Notes

a. "Damit steht die Urfrage des Menschen nach dem Grund seines Daseins unabweisbar vor ihm."

b. "Gott will nicht, daß ich schreibe, ich aber, ich muß."

c. "So sehr war ihm an (der Botschaft) gelegen, daß er sich sie noch ins Ohr wiedersagen ließ."

d. "Du aber sitzt an deinem Fenster und erträumst sie (die Botschaft) dir, wenn der Abend kommt."

e. "K. war untröstlich über die Lage des Künstlers, er begann zu weinen und schluchzte lange in die vorgehaltenen Hände."

f. "Es ist aus gelblichgrauem, gewissermaßen holzfarbigen Stoff und ist ein wenig mit Troddeln oder knopfartigen Behängen von gleicher Farbe versehen..."

g. "Den Eindruck, den ihre Hand auf mich macht, kann ich nur wiedergeben, wenn ich sage, daß ich noch keine Hand gesehen habe, bei der die einzelnen Finger derart scharf voneinander abgegrenzt wären, wie bei der ihren; doch hat ihre Hand keineswegs irgendeine anatomische Merkwürdigkeit, es ist eine völlig normale Hand."

h. "Auch liegt ja, wenn man will, eine gewisse Verantwortung auf mir, denn so fremd mir die kleine Frau auch ist, und so sehr die einzige Beziehung, die zwischen uns besteht, der Ärger ist, den ich ihr bereite, oder vielmehr der Ärger, den sie sich von mir bereiten läßt, dürfte es mir doch nicht gleichgültig sein, wie sie sichtbar unter diesem Ärger auch körperlich leidet."

i. "Vielleicht hofft sie sogar, daß wenn die Öffentlichkeit einmal ihren vollen Blick auf mich richtet, ein allgemeiner öffentlicher Ärger gegen mich entstehen und mit seinen großen Machtmitteln mich bis zur vollständigen Endgültigkeit viel kräftiger und schneller richten wird, als es ihr verhältnismäßig doch schwacher privater Ärger imstande ist; dann aber wird sie sich zurückziehen, aufatmen und mir den Rücken kehren."

j. "Was aber mit dem Dasein der kleinen Frau in sein Leben eingebrochen ist, was sich fast wie eine Wunde, die er verdeckt halten muß, an seinem Körper geöffnet hat, das hat doch im Laufe der Zeit einen unberuhigenden Charakter angenommen."

k. "Sie tritt als das absolut Andersartige, Unerklärliche in die uneigentliche Welt des bloßen Fortkommens und der Achtbarkeit ein."

l. "Die Hundegeschichte ist für das Verständnis der Gestalt des reinen Ichs in Kafkas Werk von allergrößter Bedeutung."

m. "Während Kafka in den anderen Erzählungen immer ein spezifisches Problem behandelt, verbreitet er sich in den *Forschungen* ... über den ganzen Bereich des geistigen Lebens: die Wahrheit, die Problematik der Wissenschaft, die Frage des Fortschritts, die Kunst und die Bedeutung der Religion, ihrer kultischen Form (Tanz und Gesang) wie ihrer theoretischen Systematisierung (die Musikwissenschaft)."

n. "als sei ich selbst einer der Musikanten, während ich doch nur ihr Opfer war..." (BK 184).

o. "Es fällt mir nicht ein, mich in die wahre Wissenschaft zu mengen, ich habe alle Ehrfurcht vor ihr, die ihr gebührt, aber sie zu vermehren fehlt es mir an Wissen und Fleiß und Ruhe und, nicht zuletzt, besonders seit einigen Jahren auch an Appetit" (BK 188).

p. "Alles Wissen, die Gesamtheit aller Fragen und aller Antworten ist in den Hunden enthalten" (BK 190).

q. "Und es zeigt sich dabei zwar nicht die Wahrheit — niemals wird man so weit kommen — , aber doch etwas von der tiefen Verwirrung der Lüge" (BK 195).

r. "Hatte ich nicht diese Verlassenheit gewollt? Wohl, ihr Hunde, aber nicht so hier zu enden, sondern um zur Wahrheit hinüber zu kommen aus dieser Welt der Lüge" (BK 211).

s. "Aber schon flog ich, von der Melodie gejagt, in den herrlichsten Sprüngen dahin" (BK 213).

t. "Es gibt für uns zweierlei Wahrheit, sowie sie dargestellt wird durch den Baum der Erkenntnis und den Baum des Lebens. Die Wahrheit des Tätigen und die Wahrheit des Ruhenden. In der ersten teilt sich das Gute vom Bösen, die zweite ist nichts anderes als das Gute selbst, sie weiß weder vom Guten noch vom Bösen. Die erste Wahrheit ist uns wirklich gegeben, die zweite nur ahnungsweise. Das ist der traurige Anblick. Der fröhliche ist, daß die erste Wahrheit dem Augenblick, die zweite der Ewigkeit gehört, deshalb verlischt auch die erste Wahrheit im Licht der zweiten."

3

The Apotheosis of the Artist

THE DISPLACEMENT OF the writer and human being Franz Kafka by the fiction which conveys not lies, but the truth about this person is described in one of his letters to Milena Jesenská with whom he had a brief but intimate affair (a literary, not sexual one) in the last years of his life.[1] "You forget, Milena," he wrote, "that we're really standing side by side watching this being which is me down on the ground; but in that case I who am looking am then without being."[2] In this statement Kafka implies that, while his work survives, the author himself has vanished. The fate which Kafka assigns to himself in the metaphor is the duplicate of that of the hunger artist. Commentators have established that the concept of the hunger artist itself has its origin in fact; Kafka has once again in his fiction made use of a figure borrowed from the world of vaudeville or the circus side-show who intrigued that part of the public with especially morbid interests by letting them look upon a man in the process of starving himself to death. Like the trapeze acrobat and the bareback rider he symbolizes the artist who exists in the most poignant and extreme state of outsiderness; it is pertinent in this regard to consider the fact that the word "Künstler" applies to a larger group of performers appearing before the public than does the designation "artist." (In a similar situation, the German "Dichter," a word which distinguishes, among writers, the master from the craftsman — "Schriftsteller," has no equivalent in English.) In portraying the death throes of the writer who has been sent forth to ferret out the truth in the realm of lies, Kafka has produced with "Ein Hungerkünstler" what consensus deems to be

---

[1] In another letter to Milena, he proposes that his letters themselves constitute an almost equally suitable vehicle for the conveyance of truth; he writes: "As it happens my letters are true or at least approaching truth...."[1] [[1]See Franz Kafka, *Letters to Milena*, trans., intro. by Philip Boehm (New York: Schocken, 1990), p. 219.]

[2] Ibid., p. 108.

one of his finest stories.[3] The choice of the central metaphor, the bizarre figure of the hunger artist, testifies both to Kafka's ingenuity as a creative artist and the consistency of the imagery through which he depicted his troubled life and the missionary zeal with which he pursued his literary career. The motif of food and its implications already has an important function in "Die Verwandlung." What to feed the metamorphosed Gregor concerns his mother and, principally, his sister. For his part the human "roach" first finds himself repulsed by whatever items they have selected from their store; he becomes faintly interested in the leavings from the table which his sister eventually puts down for him in his room or cell. In the final stage of his disintegration he has no appetite at all. In contrast to the starving outcast, the story's narrator shows his family, together with three boarders whom they have taken into their home in order to garner some additional income, at the dinner table, enjoying an ample meal. (They digest it while listening to a musical presentation, the violin played by Gregor's sister.) There is also in "Die Verwandlung" a final scene following the penultimate one of Gregor's death and the disposal of his body or shell by the family cook which, in a sense, presages the end of "Ein Hungerkünstler." On an outing, away from the apartment in which these dire events have occurred, the family seems to have recovered completely from their recent trials and tribulations; the strife-wearied daughter is, as the narrator reports, in particularly good health. Like the panther who replaces the hunger artist in his cage, she represents lust for life. The same enthusiasm for life-sustaining food on the part of those who disdain the protagonist and his interests makes an appearance on the pages of *Amerika* or, as Kafka himself called it, *Der Verschollene* (*One Who Vanished*); in the Hotel Occidental scene, a buffet lunch takes on the proportions of an orgiastic feast. In quite another frame of reference, the novel's protagonist, unsure of his identity, tries in vain to keep in his possession a trunk containing a few mementos of home, among them a sausage; it is stolen from him and eaten by others. It remains to be mentioned that the symbolic

---

[3] See, for example, Ingeborg Henel, "Periodisierung und Entwicklung" in *Kafka Handbuch II*, p. 239: "The objectivity of the presentation, the carefully calibrated structure, the balance between hunger and life, the compression of a difficult problem into a (single) paradox, and the depiction of the paradox as a metaphor make the *Hunger-Artist* a summit in Kafka's development, (the like of) which he has reached in none of his other more substantial works." ("Die Objektivität der Erzählweise, die Ausgewogenheit der Struktur, das Gleichgewicht von Hungern und Leben, die Verdichtung eines schwierigen Problems zum Paradox und die Darstellung des Paradoxes durch eine Metapher machen den *Hungerkünstler* zu einem Höhepunkt in Kafkas Entwicklung, den er in keinem seiner anderen größeren Werke erreicht hat.")

presentation of overeating and lack of appetite in "Ein Hungerkünstler" has autobiographical significance in regard to Kafka who not only
was a vegetarian but also abstained from drinking coffee, tea, and
alcoholic beverages. The distaste he experienced at the thought of the
overconsumption — perhaps at the mere consumption — of food
comes to light especially in one of the *Landarzt* stories, "Jackals and
Arabs" ("Schakale und Araber"). Here a traveller somewhat like the
one in "In der Strafkolonie" is called upon to rid the world of Arabs
who slaughter animals for food; however, the petitioner who makes
this plea is one of a pack of jackals, caught up but moments later in a
bloodthirsty attack on a dead camel. In "Ein Hungerkünstler" (note
that the title indicates a prototypal, not one particular character) Kafka
has taken the circus performer or "freak" who exists or used to exist
— though rarely — in reality and converted him almost completely
into a very complex symbol. The kind of truth he wishes to convey to
the reader about this figure in his story is of a non-referential order;
therefore, the nature of his act and the circumstances surrounding his
feat of fasting are pertinent only in regard to their symbolic value and
not at all to the accuracy of Kafka's portrayal of the circus milieu.
Basically the question of whether or not the hunger artist was at one
time a popular attraction needs to be addressed only in the light of
whom Kafka meant his protagonist to represent. The supposition that
the narrative has autobiographical import can all too readily be
affirmed; not only did Kafka profess in letters and journals that he had
patterned some of his protagonists after himself, but he also gave them
names, when obliged to do so, which connected them with himself.
Reasons for his having strayed from this course in developing his
fiction can hardly be imagined. It is also obvious or would seem to be
that in dealing with the life of an artist who performs for an audience
he was describing his own relationship with the public, that of a writer
with his readers.

Recent interpretations of "Ein Hungerkünstler," particularly those
by Richard Sheppard and Roy Pascal, have, although they do not
abandon completely exploring the connection between the narrative
and Kafka's plight as an artist, provided a reading which changes the
emphasis usually placed on the hunger artist's tragic death. Mention
must be made of the fact that these two critiques are not interrelated;
that is, Pascal was unaware of Sheppard's article, which had been the
first of the two to be published.[4] Both base their interpretations on a
previously unexamined feature of the story: the presence in it of a
narrator with a bias, formidable enough to cause him to be considered

[4] See Pascal, *Kafka's Narrators*, p. 244n.

another character in "Ein Hungerkünstler." A narrator who is deluded
by the protagonist into accepting the latter's self-aggrandizement as
fact has been injected into the plot, according to Sheppard, in order to
enlarge the scope of the story's theme. "It is probably better to regard
the *Hunger Artist* not as an allegory of anything," he maintains, "but
as a symbol of a psychological (or perhaps more exactly, a meta-psych-
ological) state which is not peculiar to artists and divines of all eras."[5]
For Roy Pascal, the introduction of a narrator who is unreliable
because he himself is a showman, akin to the story's impresario,
interested only in the success of the artist's performance, indicates
Kafka's resolve to give his account an ironic twist. Pascal suggests:
"The conflict between the two, both within the hunger artist and the
narrator, turns the scene into a magnificent grotesque comedy...."[6] The
lack of the impartiality which otherwise characterizes all of the
storytellers in Kafka's third-person tales is substantiated in these
readings of "Ein Hungerkünstler" by references to the anomaly of his
utterances in awkward or antiquated German and his failure to
comprehend any of the many nuances of the hunger artist's situation.
It seems to me that the significance of the figure of the unreliable
narrator lies not so much in his contributing a comic note to this
unhappy parable or in his providing yet another dimension to the
theme it displays; rather, the new kind of recognition afforded him
tends in my judgment to reaffirm, by and large, conclusions drawn
now and previously by interpreters who find in the hunger artist a
symbol for the tragic fate of the artist in recent times.[7]

The crucial function that the presence of an unreliable narrator
would have to have, in my understanding, would be to serve as a
double for the impresario. The latter is, as the fact that he is not
named, but only designated by his occupation attests, the intermediary
between the hunger artist and the public. At an important turning
point in the performer's career, he dismisses his booking agent and
manager; when he disappears from the scene, it seems clear that Kafka
has allowed the "personalized" narrator to take over his role. The

---

[5] Richard W. Sheppard, "Kafka's *Ein Hungerkünstler*: A Reconsideration," *The German Quarterly*, 46 (1973), 227.

[6] Pascal, *Kafka's Narrators*, p. 123.

[7] See, for example, Hillmann, *Franz Kafka*, p. 109: "'A Hunger Artist' is the ultimate formulation of the artist's fate" ("'Ein Hungerkünstler' ist die äußerste Gestaltung des Schicksals des Künstlers"). Even Pascal concedes that the story has great depth: "It seems to me, then, that the personalization of the narrator of 'A hunger artist' suggests a deeper reflection upon the complexity of life and suffering, of judgments, of verdicts, than we find in the earlier works of Kafka" (*Kafka's Narrators*, p. 134).

essential part he plays in the story consists of his bringing it to a close, for he reports events which occur after the hunger artist's death, including the climactic one of the replacement of the exhibit of the fasting man by the exhibit of the ravenous panther. The doubling which occurs in "Ein Hungerkünstler" is not without precedent in the Kafka canon; K.'s two assistants in *Das Schloß*, the two celluloid balls in "Blumfeld, ein älterer Junggeselle" ("Blumfeld, an Elderly Bachelor"), and, to a considerable extent, Robinson and Delamarch in *Amerika* are prominent examples of the use of this device in Kafka's fiction. Both the impresario and the narrator show sympathy for the person who apparently has been impelled to perform a strange and difficult task in the public arena, but they understand neither the significance of his act nor the nature of the torment he inflicts on himself. In this regard the two represent the members of the society, the common lot of people, within which and in relation to which the artist makes his presentation. For the public, art which claims to have a higher purpose than that of entertaining an audience or of diverting their attention away very briefly from their quotidian cares and responsibilities lies in an extraneous area of their lives. (Obviously, the impresario whose livelihood is earned by providing entertainment for the masses has for this reason more concern for the artist's tribulations than they do.)

An important factor in an interpretation of "Ein Hungerkünstler" concerns the narrator's assertion that the hunger artist had been a popular attraction and that the importance of his performance had gradually faded; the decline in the attention paid by the public to him had also directly affected the impresario's life since his client had been forced to dismiss him and appear unheralded in a lowly circus. The downfall of the protagonist in the story, a situation which only causes him to refine his artistry to the extent that he like the officer in "In der Strafkolonie" executes himself, constitutes the narrative's plot. Therefore, the relationship between the artist and the public is the central feature of "Ein Hungerkünstler," the core around which its theme develops. Kafka has previously expressed his views on this subject from the vantage point of a much more sophisticated character, that of the traveller and observer in the penal colony. Required in a very subtle way to pass judgment on a system of laws so stringent that they must be violated and punishment meted out, the visitor to the penal colony can but condemn this kind of justice, especially since every conviction incurs a death sentence. In reaching his (and the obvious) conclusions the traveller has first had to contend with the arguments in favor of proclaiming human beings guilty on all counts put to him by the officer in command of the execution machine. The points he makes resemble to a considerable degree those advanced by the hunger artist on his own behalf. Both speak for the overcoming of mortal error, for transcendence into a realm of absolute morality, one that separates the good from the evil and truth from lies by wielding an axe (cf. "Ein Landarzt"), and maintain that breaking free of the chains of mortality and mistaken identity can only be accomplished by those who sacrifice themselves for the sake of others. Thus every one who has ever died on an execution machine has after a time of intense suffering experienced a moment of triumph. The look of transcendence which appears on the face of the dying victim on the instrument of execution has in a bygone age inspired those who have come to be witnesses to this act symbolizing the vindication of the human spirit. In particular, as the narrator of "In der Strafkolonie" relates, the children watching the scene of torture — they were placed as close as possible to it — benefited from their presence at the time of the dying man's transfiguration.[8] Kafka makes use of this motif once more in "Ein Hungerkünstler"; the narrator, in describing the time of the hunger artist's success, points out: "Now it was especially the children to whom the hunger artist was shown" ("Nun waren es besonders die Kinder, denen der Hungerkünstler gezeigt wurde," 191).

There are, however, several important differences between the story Kafka wrote in the World War I years and the one he wrote at the end of his life. The character of the traveller whose viewpoint most probably represents Kafka's at the time of the writing — he is the central figure in "In der Strafkolonie" — manifestly fails to be convinced by the officer's argument that death on the machine brings about the triumph of the human spirit. Furthermore, the officer's attempt at self-sacrifice is foiled by the malfunctioning of the instrument (instrumentality) by means of which he sought to inspire and instruct others. The apparatus, and it is expressly that, paradoxically symbolizes a mechanistic age, one in which people let their lives be regulated by things which function but have no meaning. Since the traveller rather than the officer of the execution is the true protagonist, his opinion prevails that the retrogressive world of the Old Commandant was far from a better world than the materialistic one from which he has come; in addition, he discountenances the concept of the execution machine which puts a higher value on a meaningful death than it does on a full, but flawed life. Significantly, he makes his decision to flee the colony for his own sake and in his flight to freedom leaves behind his two companions.

---

[8] These motifs, it seems to me, are strikingly similar to those Shirley Jackson employs in her celebrated story "The Lottery."

The turning point in the hunger artist's story occurs when he realizes that his performance no longer matters to those whom it was intended to enlighten. His awareness of the tenuousness of his hold on the public's attention had already been a factor in his life and the manner in which he conducted his fasting; he had used all his resources in a vain effort to convince everyone, even his manager, that starving himself to the point of insensibility was not an illusion, a trick, but fact; it was indeed the only means by which he could conceivably disembody the consciousness of self in order to reach its timeless dimension. Therefore, the clock which is the only furnishing in his cage or cell does not signify, as his detractors would have it, his need to set a limit to his fast but rather his desire to outdistance time and to ascend to the realm of the immutable. Undeniably, consistency prevails in Kafka's use of imagery to indicate the close association between the artist's (writer's) aspiration to create something perceptible to all others, that is, to pass on a message, and the public's unwillingness to accept art as anything else but a random form of entertainment. Thus, in "In der Strafkolonie" the dull-witted soldier who has been placed spread-eagled on the execution machine is routinely provided with a dish of gruel which he begins as best as he can to devour. Previously, the condemned man had vomited as the officer had fastened him to the "bed" of the machine; in disgust the executioner had railed against the new commandant for allowing the women who serve him to provide food and sweets for the man condemned to death. What is implied in this sequence of events is that, in accord with Kafka's juxtaposition of life as a physical entity and death as transfiguration, food is an impediment standing in the way of spiritual transformation.

Here again the symbolism of "In der Strafkolonie" overlaps that in "Ein Hungerkünstler"; after his fasting for forty days comes to an end,[9] a ceremony celebrating the artist and his accomplishment takes place (cf. "Ein Landarzt"). The performer exhausted almost to the point of insensibility is placed by the impresario in the hands of women who are waiting to give him sustenance. The narrator describes the scene in a style which I regard to be more closely related to that of "Einsinnigkeit," the reporting of the protagonist's thoughts and feelings, rather than it is to an ironic point of view. The storyteller begins this part of his narrative with a question: "Why did this crowd (of people) who pretended to admire him so much, have so little

---

[9] The number forty obviously has a religious connotation; it occurs in both the Old and the New Testament. In the latter case it pertains to the period of time spent by Christ in the desert in preparation for the carrying out of his mission.

patience with him; if he could endure going on with his fasting, why couldn't they endure (the sight of) it (as well)? He was also tired, was comfortable sitting in the straw, and was now supposed to stand up tall and straight and go to eat (a meal) the very idea of which made him nauseated, (a condition) which he suppressed with some effort in consideration of the women (present). And he looked up into the eyes of the apparently very friendly ladies, who were in reality so awful, and shook his head, too heavy for his weak neck (to hold upright)."[a] Unlike the traveller in the earlier story, the hunger artist does not decide that the concept of art's edifying function realized at the cost of the victimization of the artist is unacceptable. He resigns himself to his fate: "Now the hunger artist endured it all" ("Nun duldete der Hungerkünstler alles"), the narrator testifies; he also reports that the manager calls his artist "a pitiful martyr" (although he suggests that the impresario is not too sure of what he means).

The resolve of the hunger artist to continue his exhibition of fasting clashes, as he comes to see, with a sharp decline in the public's interest in such a performance. In order to shore up his claim that his artistic exploit is truly a matter of bringing enlightenment to humanity, he dismisses the impresario who has given his feat the aura of a vaudeville act and joins a circus where he can be exhibited in his cage like the animals that so easily capture the public's attention. When he finds, as he soon does, that this strategy does not work, he decides, very much in the manner of the officer of the execution, to sacrifice himself in order to establish the validity of his mission; he will engage in the perfect fast, one that has no end (but the obvious one).[10] But he is thwarted in every aspect of his enterprise as a circus performer. The significance of his fasting beyond the usual limit of forty days is lost when circus personnel fail to post the number of days which have elapsed since his act of hungering began. In his recognition of the ongoing indifference of the public the hunger artist finds it particularly painful that the children who sometimes pause on their way to the

---

[10] Bert Nagel points out that the artist's search for perfection, for the ultimate form of expression, leads, particularly in Kafka's case, to the transformation of the real into the grotesque; he posits: "The very fact that in Kafka's work the artist is depicted as a hunger artist, a circus acrobat, a bareback rider, or the female mouse Josefine as a singer, or even in the form of a mole-like forest creature, places art and the artist in a macabre light and designates artistic achievement as an eccentric act or as fanatical foolishness," *Franz Kafka* (Berlin: Erich Schmidt, 1974), p. 211. ("Schon die Tatsache, daß in Kafkas Dichtungen der Künstler im Bild eines Hungerkünstlers, eines Zirkusartisten, einer Kunstreiterin, oder der Mäusin Josefine als Sängerin, oder sogar in der Gestalt eines maulwurfähnliches Waldtieres vorgestellt wird, rückt Kunst und Künstlertum in ein makabres Licht und kennzeichnet künstlerische Leistung als Exzentrik oder fanatische Narretei.")

wild animal exhibit and peer into his cage are even more lackadaisical than their parents. The fasting man who is on the verge of dying in order to show them the way to a spirituality which will ennoble their lives laments the lack of education which prevails in the contemporary world and tries to locate in the children's eyes a hope for the future (which he will not see himself): "The children were still uncomprehending because of their insufficient education in school and life — what did they know of hunger? — yet they revealed in the glow of their searching eyes something about a new age, a coming, more gracious age."[b] Resigning himself to his fate, his dying without having carried out his mission, he acknowledges the irony which underlies his situation in the cage; here he attracts the momentary attention of those whose goal it is to revel in the sight of the ravenous wild animals housed just beyond his exhibit.

The hunger artist's last confrontation is with one of the zoo-keepers. Peering into the cage's dusty straw, the roustabout at first cannot locate the performer's emaciated body; when he does, he puts his ear to the bars of the cage in order to hear the feeble voice of the death-bound man inside. The gesture is a familiar one in the Kafka canon; it occurs most prominently in the parable "Vor dem Gesetz." There it is the doorkeeper who bends down so that he can catch the last words of the man from the country; the voyager who has come many years previously to seek admittance to the law asks almost inaudibly why no one but him has tried to enter through this particular gate. The doorkeeper informs him with an undertone of irony that it was an entrance for him and him alone and could now be shut. The conversation between the hunger artist and the circus worker has the same satiric bent, but the more bitter irony underlies the remarks of the moribund man. He seems to denigrate his life's work, his search for truth or self-knowledge undertaken for the sake of passing the wisdom he has garnered on to others. He has fasted, he confesses to the roustabout, because he could not find any food which he wanted to eat. This particular comment has led some interpreters of "Ein Hungerkünstler" to reject the formerly widely accepted reading of the story as an exposition of the artist's tragic lot, his recognition of his own inadequacy and the inadequacy of the means he employs to reach the world of absolutes beyond reality.[11] An alternative reading of the hunger artist's final comment on the import of his fasting would propose that the paradoxical element ubiquitous in Kafka's fiction

---

[11] See, for example, Hillmann, *Franz Kafka*, p. 109: "'A Hunger Artist' is the gloomiest projection of the artist's fate" ("'Ein Hungerkünstler' ist die düsterste Gestaltung des Schicksals des Künstlers").

prevails even here; the artist realizes at the end of his career not only that his self-sacrifice has been in vain but also that it has been a deception in which he has indulged himself and by which he has tried to dazzle and betray the public. In a letter to Max Brod, written on July 5, 1922, Kafka expressed sentiments in regard to his writing which approach the negativity some critics find implicit in the story's ending. Kafka states: "Writing is a sweet, wonderful reward, but for what? ... The reward for serving the devil.... This descent to dark powers, this freeing of spirits enchained by nature (and) of dubious embraces, of whatever else may take place down below, about which one (back) on the surface no longer knows, as one writes (one's) stories in the sunlight. Perhaps there is another kind of writing, (but) I know only this (kind).... And the devilish (element) in all of this seems very clear to me. It is the vanity and enjoyment which always swirls around one's or someone else's figure and takes pleasure in it...."[12c] On a previous occasion in "Ein Hungerkünstler" the protagonist has already permitted himself to give vent to his desire for adulation; he berates the people passing by his cage for their indifference — he calls it malicious disregard — to his plight. "The hunger artist was not deceptive," the narrator reports; "he worked with integrity. But the world cheated him of his reward."[d]

This slight fall from grace, a moment of self-indulgence, I would propound, is relived by the hunger artist with perhaps greater intensity as he draws his dying breath; it is noteworthy that the narrator cancels out the substance of the performer's complaint that he could never find a food to suit his taste with the comment: "But still in his broken eyes there was the firm, if no longer prideful conviction that his fast was continuing."[e] In addition to this affirmative note, the story ends with a coda which also tends to confirm the supposition that Kafka did not depart in "Ein Hungerkünstler" from his usual seriousness of purpose in depicting the travail of the artist-writer. The last paragraph portrays the intellectual's nemesis in the guise of a voracious panther that replaces the hunger artist in his cage. The narrator commends the animal for the naturalness of his appetite and in that respect attributes to the beast a lust for life ("Freude am Leben"). Unlike the artist and aesthete, the panther can revel in the freedom to be himself. His unabashed animality, the fervor with which he devours raw meat, holds the visitors to the circus entranced in a way that the hunger artist never could.

The message he leaves behind him after his last self-destructive fast falls mostly on deaf ears; only a random few who passed by during his

[12] Kafka, *Briefe 1902-1924*, p. 384 f.

quest for martyrdom may have grasped intuitively the significance of the artist's pursuit of self-knowledge, obtainable only by transcending the physical realm of existence. Hillmann's discussion of the story makes the point succinctly: "(Society) thus learns clearly what it has forgotten in its everyday life and its superficial need for distraction, namely that an essential and necessary factor of human existence is the unrestricted search for truth."[13] In the last of the four stories collected under the title of *Ein Hungerkünstler*, "Josefine die Sängerin oder das Volk der Mäuse," the role of the public in relation to that of the artist as a purveyor of truth is subjected to close examination.

---

[13] Hillmann, *Franz Kafka*, p. 90; the quotation reads: "(Die Gesellschaft) erfährt so deutlich, was sie über ihrem Alltagsleben und ihrem leichtsinnigen Rummelbedürfnis vergessen hat, daß nämlich ein wesentliches und notwendiges Moment des menschlichen Daseins die unbedingte Suche nach der Wahrheit ist").

Notes

a. "Warum hatte diese Menge, die ihn so sehr zu bewundern vorgab, so wenig Geduld mit ihm; wenn er es aushielt, noch weiter zu hungern, warum wollte sie es nicht aushalten? Auch war er müde, saß gut im Stroh und sollte sich nun hoch und lang aufrichten und zu dem Essen gehn, das ihm schon allein in der Vorstellung Übelkeiten verursachte, deren Äußerung er nur mit Rücksicht auf die Damen mühselig unterdrückte. Und er blickte empor in die Augen der scheinbar so freundlichen, in Wirklichkeit so grausamen Damen und schüttelte den auf dem schwachen Halse überschweren Kopf" (194).

b. "Die Kinder (blieben) wegen ihre ungenügenden Vorbereitung von Schule und Leben her zwar immer noch verständnislos — was war ihnen Hungern? — aber (verrieten) doch in dem Glanz ihrer forschenden Augen etwas von neuen, kommenden, gnädigeren Zeiten" (199).

c. "Das Schreiben ist ein süßer wunderbarer Lohn, aber wofür? ... Der Lohn für Teufelsdienst.... Dieses Hinabgehen zu den dunklen Mächten, diese Entfesselung von Natur aus gebundener Geister, fragwürdiger Umarmungen und was alles noch unten vor sich gehen mag, von dem man oben nichts mehr weiß, wenn man im Sonnenlicht Geschichten schreibt. Vielleicht gibt es auch anderes Schreiben, ich kenne nur dieses.... Und das Teuflische daran scheint mir sehr klar. Es ist die Eitelkeit und Genußsucht, die immerfort um die eigene oder auch an eine fremde Gestalt ... schwirrt und sie genießt...."

d. "Nicht der Hungerkünstler betrog, er arbeitete ehrlich, aber die Welt betrog ihn um seinen Lohn" (199).

e. "Aber noch in seinen gebrochenen Augen war die feste, wenn auch nicht mehr stolze Überzeugung, daß er weiterhungere" (200).

4

A Message from "We the People"

KAFKA FIRST TITLED his story (it was to be his last) "Josefine die Sängerin" and only later added "oder das Volk der Mäuse" ("Josefine — or Josephine — the Songstress or the Mouse People"), in order, he proposed, to strike a balance. It is a most provocative title. Even before it announces that the story will take the form of an animal fable it provides the information that the protagonist is to be a woman, specifically a woman artist. This factor in the fiction, which is of an exceptional nature in the Kafka canon, has been all but overlooked by most commentators; perhaps they have assumed all too readily that the name Josef(ine) identifies the character as having an autobiographical basis (Kafka is Josef K.'s amanuensis in *Der Prozeß*) and also a historical one since the biblical Joseph with his coat of many colors and his ability to interpret dreams symbolizes the artist. Only recently have a few critics — Ruth Gross in particular — emphasized the deliberateness of Kafka's choice of a female protagonist.[1] In her article Ruth Gross posits that the twofold use of the feminine noun suffix "in" places the hero(ine!) of the story in an unfavorable light, particularly when she stands alone as a counterpart to "das Volk," all other people. Providing an answer to the question of why Kafka chose to present yet another portrait of the artist but with a surprising difference, that of the gender of the protagonist, Gross posits: "By an ancient topos, woman is music, while man is poetry, woman ineffable, man articulate...."[2] Linguistically in regard to "Josefine," a preponderance of instances of the association of art with the feminine lies close at hand: most obvious is the fact that the word "art" itself is "die Kunst" in German. Of particular importance, since it represents a key symbol in Kafka's work, is the word "music," which is "die Musik"; furthermore,

---

[1] See Ruth Gross, "Of Mice and Women: Reflections on a Discourse" in *Franz Kafka: His Craft and Thought*, ed. Roman Struc & J. C. Yardley (Waterloo, Canada: Wilfrid Laurier University Press, 1986), 117-140.

[2] Ibid., p. 129.

the patron saint of music is a woman, Saint Cecilia.[3] There is also indisputably a self-depreciatory element in Kafka's fiction which most often takes the form of the portrayal of the protagonist's submissiveness, his weakness, in contrast to the aggressiveness of his adversaries. In choosing the format of the animal fable for the last of the four stories in the *Ein Hungerkünstler* collection (the other three deal with human beings), Kafka gave himself the opportunity not only to describe himself as the lowliest and weakest of creatures, notably *"die Maus,"* but also the kind whose presence even in smaller numbers he found intolerable. In essence, "Josefine, die Sängerin oder das Volk der Mäuse" is less a story (there is no plot) and more, as the title indicates, a debate on the subject of the function of art in society; the dispute ends in a tie. Both the arguments on behalf of the artist and the arguments on behalf of the unaesthetic community prevail.

Under these circumstances the role of the moderator would seem to fall to the narrator, but he does not present himself as an individual, an "I," vaguely linked to the masculine author, rather as "we," the people. Mention must be made of the fact that the German word "das Volk," which has a neuter, non-gender aspect, has implications beyond those of its English equivalent. Also, the association of "folk" with plain people, as in "folklore" and "folk song," does not adequately indicate the mythic undertone with which "das Volk" resounds. Feasibly some indication of this depth of meaning can be obtained by a reference to the double-rendering in German of the concept of "society." The two German equivalents are "die Gesellschaft" and "die Gemeinschaft"; a number of interpreters of "Josefine" have therefore and, given Kafka's concern for the ethnic interests of the Jewish people, with good reason equated the society of mice with the Jewish community in Europe in the first quarter of the twentieth century. However, taking this subtext and bringing it to the forefront seems to me to provide a reading which is untrue to the nature of the story. Demonstrably, Kafka uses the animal fable in order to make an argument; otherwise, in depicting human beings in his fiction, he transmits as a rule an experience to the reader.[4] It is therefore the function of the narrator to present the collective opinion of his

---

[3] Kafka was surely familiar with a story by an author he admired and probably sought at least at times to emulate, Kleist's "Die heilige Cäcilie oder die Gewalt der Musik" ("Saint Cecilia or the Power of Music"); note the twofold aspect of the title.

[4] See Pascal, *Kafka's Narrators*, p. 172: "While in the stories and novels the reader is offered only the experience of the hero, in the parables he is directed towards reflections about events; in the first his objective is experience, in the second it is knowledge, understanding."

contemporaries about the phenomenon, Josefine's singing, with which they are confronted in their otherwise humdrum lives. At the same time he — giving the narrator that gender as a matter of convenience — is called upon to devise a rationale for her performance. As Ruth Gross propounds, the self-appointed representative of the populace has the difficult task of creating "a character who is both more or less than himself."[5] In carrying out this endeavor, he employs the method which duplicates that of Kafka in devising his fiction: a series of propositions or happenings are presented, the substantiality of which is subsequently undermined. In other words, the truth is sought after by the invention of a fictitious world which exposes the lies or half-truths in the real world.

In this wise the storyteller begins his narrative with a series of assertions which appear to be statements of fact: "Our songstress is named Josefine. Anyone who has not heard her (sing), does not know the power of song. There is no one who isn't carried away by her singing, (a conclusion) which must have even greater value since our society doesn't in general love music."[a] Gradually the narrator downgrades Josefine's singing to the point of insisting that she has no vocal talent at all.[6] The people's representative quickly begins to question the value of Josefine's contribution to the mouse society. "In intimate circles," he professes, "we confess to one another openly that Josefine's singing as singing is not at all extraordinary."[b] He associates her vocal performance with the piping (Pascal calls it "cheeping") that all mice engage in and adds that she even does it less well than the average mouse. His viewpoint can readily be equated with that of most people when confronted with works of art which exist primarily for their aesthetic value — for example, opera, the ballet, abstract painting, poetry. Such artistic accomplishments strike the general public as they do the narrator to be wildly exaggerated forms of ordinary behavior. Thereby, operatic singing is the product of an abnormal use of the voice, that is, speech fashioned into something unintelligible. The link between Josefine and the hunger artist, as well as Kafka's other protagonists, comes into view from this vantage point. All are ordinary people with ordinary talents which they have chosen (or been chosen) to develop to the uttermost refinement. In the

[5] Gross, "Of Mice and Women," p. 132.

[6] Robertson, whose book *Kafka: Judaism, Politics, and Literature* deals most knowledgeably with Kafka's concerns as a Jewish writer, seems to have taken this aspect of Josefine's story too literally; he draws the conclusion that her lack of talent in the field of music is in actuality the rule in the Jewish community and writes of "their relative lack of interest in music" (p. 283).

instance of the hunger artist, so to speak, Kafka's vegetarianism has been elevated to the rank of an esoteric feat, or, rather more specifically, his writing has been given the aura of a mission. The narrator in "Josefine" like the canine researcher is led to explore the aesthetic dimension in life, for he concludes that, if Josefine's talent is non-existent in the realm of reality, he must seek to discover the nature of the power she exerts over society. "If this were all true," he proposes in regard to her prideful claim to possess a talent which is in truth no more than an ability to perform a simple function of mice, "then the supposed artistry of Josefine would be repudiated, but (at the same time) it would be most appropriate to solve the riddle of the great influence (she exerts)."[c]

The first approach the prototypal mouse makes toward finding an answer to the enigma of aesthetic experience focusses on the question of the nature of art. Himself a symbol, he conceives of a symbol which will afford an explanation. He supposes that there was once somebody, some mouse, who cracked nuts especially well. It occurred to this individual that he (the gender is arbitrary) might demonstrate his talent in public, even though he was aware that people generally were already proficient in nut-cracking. Nevertheless, he chose to make his abilities known and appeared in the public arena. Those who witnessed his exploit were puzzled because they felt they could perform it equally well or even better. However, so the mouse narrator decides, the people witnessing the perhaps even uninspiring performance of nut-cracking were thereby driven to see an everyday event in a new light. In this sense of providing a revelation or knowledge about an overlooked aspect of life, art might serve the community. The implication is clear that Kafka had come to consider his fiction to be a message, uncovering (to use Heidegger's terminology) some overlooked aspect of life — in "Josefine" the role that the aesthetic or non-pragmatic plays in the tragicomedy of human existence.

Proceeding with his arguments pro and contra the significance of art and the artist in regard to the everyday world, the narrator next considers the impression that Josefine makes on her audience. Here, once again, the motif recurs which is such a prominent feature of the other stories in the *Hungerkünstler* collection, namely, the obsessive nature of the artist's devotion to art. Like the trapeze acrobat who requires a second swing for his performance, the anomalous storyteller who invents an enemy to carry out the machinations he has conceived of in order to torment himself, and the hunger artist who sets himself the ultimate goal of starving himself to death, Josefine demands not only that she be rewarded for her accomplishments by being exempted from all social obligations, that is, working on community projects, defending the nation when it is attacked (on such occasions she runs away and hides), but also that as a performer she be worshiped. Frustrated in this respect, as the narrator suggests, Josefine will turn on members of the community and bite; this tendency calls to mind the fantastic groom in "Ein Landarzt" who bites Rosa on the cheek and is about to inflict other injuries on her. Despite the psychopathic state in which his or her single-mindedness sometimes leaves the artist, the populace whom he or she is driven to serve does not shrink from according their aberrant member the most tender care. "So, therefore, the people look after Josefine in the way a father does who takes up a child that stretches out its hand to him — one cannot tell whether it is pleading for or demanding something," the storyteller reports.[d]

The solicitude afforded Josefine by the mouse people in a fatherly fashion represents, on Kafka's part, the putting into use in his fiction of the most radical paradox. The argument advanced by the narrator on behalf of his constituency, and it must be taken into account that it is only an argument, contends that the relationship between the artist and society is not adversarial. Indeed, Kafka seems to claim at this point in his literary career that all the impediments he had struggled to remove from the pathway leading to his goal, the fulfillment of his mission as a writer, had been illusory or at least merely transitory. His newfound hope was that the people who had forsaken the hunger artist in his cage could correct their mistake. The narrator in "Josefine" expresses the same optimism, disguised in the form of an understatement: "Her art(istry) does not go unnoticed. Although we basically are preoccupied with other things and silence prevails (in the auditorium) for a certainty not only for the sake of the singing and many a listener does not look up at all but buries his face in his neighbor's fur and Josefine seems to be toiling in vain up there (on the stage), some of the piping does, undeniably, without fail come through even to us. This piping which arises where silence has been imposed on all others, comes (through) *almost like a message from the people to the individual*; the thin (weak) piping of Josefine in the midst of difficult decisions is almost like the pitiful existence of our people in the midst of the tumult of an inimical world" (my italics).[e]

Josefine's story does not end with the presentation of this apologia for the artist's existence, but it is a striking exegesis of the relationship between art and all people (rather than a sophisticated few). Kafka appears to be facing the fantastic prospect of a society in which respect for his writing flourishes and perhaps even pictures a father who might have a change of heart. Kafka's ambition in writing to raise the sphere of the mundane into the regions of the pure, the true, the immutable has momentarily the semblance of having been absorbed into the relatively simple task of giving the least and loneliest of the community a sense of his or her share in the general lot of humanity or insight into the self of a human being. The purpose of art as this turn in the story implies is the carrying out of an artless and at the same time vital function, the establishment of a bond between the commonplace and the esoteric, the mundane and the other-worldly. The artist accordingly becomes the means through which each individual is freed for the time being but actually for all time from the chains of the drudgery of life and the vicissitudes of history. (The narrator proposes that the mice-folk has little use for historians.) Josefine's piping, whatever its true nature is, has great significance as a symbol of this process of liberation. In the final analysis, Kafka sees his writing as a vehicle which transforms the sham truth of reality into the pure truth of the abstract, the imaginative. The music which Josefine creates is nothing audible, that is, tangible, but an image in the mind. The reality of this symbol is on a par with the reality of the world external to it; in sum, referential truth has been subsumed in the concept of aesthetic truth. Expressing the viewpoint of "das Volk," the narrator describes the situation in which art becomes a part of the nature of society: "Piping is the language of our people, only many a one (of us) pipes all his life long and doesn't realize it, here (in Josefine's singing), however, our piping is freed of the shackles of daily life and in addition makes us free ourselves for a little while."[f] Critics have emphasized the importance of this climactic moment in "Josefine." Pascal states: "This paragraph is unparalleled in Kafka's work. It is a hymn to art, and significantly it is at the same time a hymn to the harmony of artist and audience, of artist and society."[7] Robertson also reaches the conclusion that in this story Kafka has reevaluated his opinions on the subject of the artist and society and gives this interpretation of the relationship between Josefine and her audience: "The 'Volk' understands art better than the artist does."[8]

Having reached this point in the contention between the claim of art and the artist to be of overwhelming significance in life and the claim of the populace to be entitled to consider the matter of sheer survival as having greater importance, the voice of the mouse people takes up the subject of Josefine's standing in the community. Although he judges her demands for particular attention to be inappropriate, he makes allowances for her having put them forth. "What she strives for," he proposes, "is therefore only the recognition of her art which

[7] Pascal, *Kafka's Narrators*, p. 227.

[8] Robertson, *Kafka: Judaism, Politics, and Literature*, p. 283.

will be publicly and unequivocally expressed, will prevail through the ages, and will rise above all previously known (kinds of recognition)."[g] This ambition attributed to Josefine by the mouse narrator can but have ironic overtones in the light of Kafka's own sense of mission. In regard to Josefine the storyteller also puts to rest the suspicion that she has become so importunate only as death nears. Her demands that her art be acclaimed, he contends, have a long history and cannot therefore be withdrawn at random. Using as so often the stylistic device of expressing reality in the subjunctive mood, Kafka lets the narrator delve into Josefine's thinking: "Perhaps she should have turned the attack upon her off in another direction in the beginning, perhaps she now can see for herself her error, but now she can no longer retreat; retreating (from her demands) would mean becoming untrue to herself; now she must stand or fall on the point of her demand(s)."[h] Kafka's own ambition to achieve perfection in his writing is reflected in this depiction of Josefine's pleading for special consideration for the artist who lives his life for art alone. The obsessiveness with which Kafka's protagonists pursue their goal is criticized in retrospect in this way by the author himself. However, in this story which contains more than a few comments which pertain to his work in a summary fashion, Kafka still seeks to justify the hyperbolic quality of the standards he set for himself in his literary pursuits. Thus, Josefine is provided with an ennobling excuse for her radical behavior: "When sie demands something, she isn't led to do that by external circumstances, but by an inner (need for) consistency. She reaches out for the highest crown, not because it is hanging low for the moment, but (simply) because it is the highest; if it were in her power, she would hang it even higher."[i]

The exposition of Josefine's point of view undertaken by the narrator on behalf of the community also makes allowance for their lack of appreciation for the artist's performance. While Kafka has in his earlier stories concerning the public's indifference to art expressed mainly the frustration on the artist's part which it effects, in "Josefine" he emphasizes the commonality of their endeavors. The trials and tribulations of the group complement those of the individual. The mockery which characterizes the immolation of the country doctor in the service of the community performed by the community itself is diminished in the mouse narrator's description of Josefine's concerts. The dire fate which awaits the hunger artist when he joins the circus and subsequently, in order to capture the attention of the general public, begins a deadly fast is spared Josefine. Her destiny calls for her simply to disappear, in a way, to transcend the struggle for recognition. At first her physical condition like that of the hunger artist deteriorates, and she can no longer sing. Although her audience accepts the disappearance of her song and then her own disappearance without comment, she has become a part of their *Gemeinschaft*, their sense of community. The narrator ends his study of the relationship between the artist and society in the evenhanded fashion in which he conducted it; he sums up the debate in which both the individual and the aggregate of human beings have asserted their rights with a question: "Didn't the people, moreover, in their wisdom put such great worth in Josefine's singing exactly because it was in this way (being more than just a memory) immutable?"[j]

The amalgamation of the individual's sense of self with the community's sense of self constitutes Kafka's exceptionally positive solution to the artist's and in particular the writer's dilemma, the disparity between the effort of the individual to rise above society's norms and the insistence on the part of society that those norms be maintained. The story ends with Josefine's disappearance into the community's consciousness, a state of self-awareness which Josefine herself has helped to bring into sharper focus. She has carried out her mission to a point at least very close to completion, and therefore the narrator proposes: "Perhaps we will not even be giving up very much (in losing Josefine)."[k] At the same time the story-teller seeks to compensate the artist somewhat for his having consigned her to oblivion; he gives her final feat of vanishing the aura of an ascension. His term for the manner of her death is "gesteigerte Erlösung," a rarefied form of salvation, release from all earthly ills. Pascal has pointed out Kafka's fondness for the word "Erlösung" (a fondness he shared with a number of contemporary writers) and defined it accordingly. Pascal posits: "(It) has many meanings in this period, from the banal 'end to suffering' to the mystic transcendence of a spiritual being that replaces man's earthly integument."[9] In suggesting that Josefine may be afforded a kind of sainthood, the narrator, neverthe-less, does not quite relinquish his role as a speaker for the community of ordinary people. He grants his constituency their share of "Er-lösung," although of a less rarefied sort, for they, too, disappear from the scenes of their daily rounds and are blessedly forgotten. In "Josefine die Sängerin oder das Volk der Mäuse" Kafka has averred with almost his last breath that he has reached the goal he had set for himself as a writer of bringing a message to the community; it revealed to them an intimation of the meaningfulness of their tedious lives. But they, in turn, so the story goes, promulgated a message for the artist, affirming their belief in the visionary nature of art.

---

[9] Pascal, *Kafka's Narrators*, p. 229.

Establishing the mutuality of the concerns of artists and their counterparts, people of no particular sophistication, is the task Kafka assigned himself as he approached the end of his life, a situation of which he was fully aware. In developing the character of the artist, his last portrait of the figure, he seems to have recognized in himself traits shaping the writer which he associated with strengths and weaknesses perceived by society as inherently feminine. Basically, the concept of mothering, of providing for the fundamental need of the social group, be it family or folk, i.e., sustenance in all forms necessary for survival, relates to a womanly preoccupation. Maintaining harmony is an important aspect of this task. Josefine defines her role in society largely in accord with such an endeavor. In "Die Verwandlung" it is the insect's sister who tries to reconcile the family to the transformation of the protagonist; even after she has given up this self-assigned task, she undertakes, by playing the violin after dinner for the three paying guests, to mend the torn fabric of family life. The assignment of this part to the sister rather than the mother in the Samsa family has, indisputably, autobiographical import. Since Kafka's mother, in order to assist her husband with his business ventures, left her children in the care of servants, Kafka considered her to be wanting in motherliness. In "Das Urteil," a story which he held in high esteem, the mother is deceased. Weakness in the physical sense but also in the sense of a lack of courage characterizes the mother in "Die Verwandlung." As a substitute mother the figure of the manageress in *Amerika* or *Der Verschollene* fails the protagonist in a time of crisis and abandons him to his fate. In the same novel Brunelda, a woman whose girth is of motherly proportions, plays a sinister role and torments the adolescent Karl Roßmann. In Kafka's lifetime his sister Ottla began to function as a motherly care-giver; in particular she provided the accommodations in which he could pursue his writing career, first a small house she owned in Prague which he had entirely to himself, later a room, meals, and even more importantly the solitude he required in the house where she and her family lived while engaged in a farming venture. Furthermore, Ottla was a model for him of womanly independence; she risked, as he never did, except for a very brief period at the end of his life, cutting herself off from parental assistance to develop her own way of life which included marriage to a non-Jew. Surely, if only to a slight extent, the portrait of the artist as a woman in "Josefine" pays tribute to Ottla's spirited taking hold of life. In contrast, although Kafka appears in the long run to have accepted his mother's lack of attention in his early years as having been unavoidable, he regarded her motherliness with a cold eye; for instance, he may well have become aware that she had written to Felice Bauer, the woman he wished to marry, without his knowledge and had even hired a detective to look into her background. Evidence of his cautious attitude toward his mother comes to light in the fact that he handed her the voluminous letter to his father, his accusatory brief in the case of Kafka contra the world, with the full expectation both that she would read it and that she would not transmit it to her husband. The symbolic reconciliation which occurs between Josefine and the mouse folk has just a suggestion of Kafka's coming to terms with his parents' indifference to his writing; they were never able to appreciate any of it.

Josefine is, of course, not the only woman character in Kafka's work who stands outside of familial relationships. In "Das Urteil" Frieda Brandenfeld appears who is the fiancée of the protagonist Georg Bendemann. As Kafka himself indicated in an attempt at interpreting his own story, she exists as a pawn in the deadly game played by father and son; both use her as a threat with which they taunt one another. Georg claims his engagement is an instrument with which he will destroy his father's authority over him; the elder Bendemann defiantly ridicules the attachment between the two. The association of F(rieda) B(randenfeld) with F(elice) B(auer) not only comes too readily to mind, but it was also sanctioned by Kafka himself. He fashioned their romance or at least contemplation of marriage into an epistolary novel; in his letters to Felice Kafka attempts to frighten her away by emphasizing the demands he will make on her as a husband, none of which, however, is of a sexual nature. Josefine's insistence on having the total attention of her audience duplicates Kafka's desire to live a life in which even marriage is subservient to his literary pursuits; her stance, however, when she is frustrated in having her way, her stomping her foot and her pouting, must be taken to be Kafka's somewhat wry portrayal of what he considered to be typically feminine behavior. Upon determining that tuberculosis (the wound) had doomed him to a celibate life, one more in accord with the destiny of a dedicated artist, Kafka was able to give up Felice Bauer as a prospective wife and to allow her image to fade from his fiction. A trace remains in the figure of Rosa in "Ein Landarzt"; it is she who has been the doctor's much neglected companion and helpmate and whom he leaves behind to ward off the attack of a predatory male. From another vantage point she becomes the victim of the doctor's abandonment as he flies off into the ethereal regions of art. In "Josefine" the woman artist has neither a family from which she comes nor a family which she aspires to found.

As much as the character Josefine seems to be, on the whole, unrelated to the women who actually played a part in Kafka's life, she is nonetheless a part of the conciliatory and positive attitude he assumes toward the fate of the artist — to be neglected by and yet taken into the fold of humanity. This affirmation of his destiny which he expressed in his darkest days can but be in great measure the result of a relationship he established with Dora Diamant (sometimes spelled Dymant), a young woman from a very orthodox Jewish family, whom he met while she was working in a vacation camp in Berlin. Her dedication to the tasks she performed for the youngsters in her charge equalled his own to his role as an artist/writer. They began living together; the poor state of his health and the financial indigencies they had to withstand (inflation and the short supply of food haunted Berlin) precluded their extending their arrangements into those of even an informal marriage. Nevertheless, Kafka was able to consider Dora to be the companion or wife he had so long sought — a sexually non-threatening Felice Bauer, a Milena Jesenská who tried neither to seduce nor mother him. She seems also not to have involved herself in his work, as Milena clearly did. Indication of Dora's reserve in this regard is her report of Kafka's making the room less cold by burning manuscripts in the stove; she apparently did not try to stop him. Together with Robert Klopstock, who, while bolstering Kafka's ambition to write, left literary matters strictly in his hands, Dora attended to the difficult assignment of making the deathly ill author as comfortable physically as at all possible in his last days. They established for him as the mouse folk established for the cantankerous Josefine that his struggle to express what was pure, true, and immutable in art had not been in vain and could be appreciated even by literarily underprivileged folk.

Notes

a. "Unsere Sängerin heißt Josefine. Wer sie nicht gehört hat, kennt nicht die Macht des Gesanges. Es gibt niemanden, den ihr Gesang nicht fortreißt, was um so höher zu bewerten ist, als unser Geschlecht im ganzen Musik nicht liebt" (200).

b. "Im vertrauten Kreise gestehen wir einander offen, daß Josefinens Gesang als Gesang nichts Außerordentliches darstellt" (201).

c. "Wenn das alles wahr wäre, dann wäre zwar Josefinens angebliche Künstlerschaft widerlegt, aber es wäre dann erst recht das Rätsel ihrer großen Wirkung zu lösen" (201).

d. "So sorgt also das Volk für Josefine in der Art eines Vaters, der sich eines Kindes annimmt, das sein Händchen — man weiß nicht recht, ob bittend oder fordernd — nach ihm ausstreckt" (205).

e. "Ihre Kunst bleibt nicht unbeachtet. Trotzdem wir im Grunde mit ganz anderen Dingen beschäftigt sind und die Stille durchaus nicht nur dem Gesange zuliebe herrscht und mancher gar nicht aufschaut, sondern das Gesicht in den Pelz des Nachbars drückt und Josefine also dort oben sich vergeblich abzumühen scheint, dringt doch — das ist nicht zu leugnen — etwas von ihrem Pfeifen unweigerlich auch zu uns. Dieses Pfeifen, das sich erhebt, wo allen anderen Schweigen auferlegt ist, kommt fast wie eine Botschaft des Volkes zu dem Einzelnen; das dünne Pfeifen Josefinens mitten in den schweren Entscheidungen ist fast wie die armselige Existenz unseres Volkes mitten im Tumult der feindlichen Welt" (207).

f. "Pfeifen ist die Sprache unseres Volkes, nur pfeift mancher sein Leben lang und weiß es nicht, hier aber ist das Pfeifen frei gemacht von den Fesseln des täglichen Lebens und befreit uns auch für eine kurze Weile" (210).

g. "Was sie anstrebt, ist also nur die öffentliche, eindeutige, die Zeiten überdauernde, über alles bisher Bekannte sich weit erhebende Anerkennung ihrer Kunst" (212).

h. "Vielleicht hätte sie den Angriff gleich anfangs in andere Richtung lenken sollen, vielleicht sieht sie jetzt selbst den Fehler ein, aber nun kann sie nicht mehr zurück, ein Zurückgehen hieße sich selbst untreu werden, nun muß sie schon mit dieser Forderung stehen oder fallen" (212).

i. "Wenn sie etwas fordert, so wird sie nicht durch äußere Dinge, sondern durch innere Folgerichtigkeit dazu gebracht. Sie greift nach dem höchsten Kranz, nicht weil er im Augenblick gerade ein wenig tiefer hängt, sondern weil es der höchste ist; wäre es in ihrer Macht, sie würde ihn noch höher hängen" (213).

j. "Hat nicht vielmehr das Volk in seiner Weisheit Josefinens Gesang, eben deshalb, weil er in dieser Art (mehr als eine bloße Erinnerung) unverlierbar war, so hoch gestellt?" (216).

k. "Vielleicht werden wir also gar nicht sehr viel entbehren" (216).

5

Kafka's Paradise Lost

MAX BROD (a more knowledgeable enthusiast for Kafka's work) who found the manuscript of a story about an unspecified animal and his burrow among Kafka's papers subsequent to his death gave it the title of "Der Bau" ("The Burrow"). He could scarcely have done otherwise since the rather lengthy narrative deals obsessively, that is, without even the suggestion of a plot, with the significance of the creature's subterranean den. However, the English translation of the title is, despite its appropriateness, deficient in that it fails to make allowance for the many nuances of the German "Bau." Primarily, the kind of construction to which it refers can exist both above the earth and in it, as well as in the form of an abstraction, without being physically present. The word's ambiguity or, rather, wide range of meaning came about because its original sense of digging — therefore, "Bauer"/"farmer"[1] — was quickly associated with the permanency of the abode of the digger. Because of the different kinds of construction conjured up by the concept of "Bau," the underground labyrinth devised by the animal[2] can have an association with many other structures featured in Kafka's fiction, be they castle, mine, law courts, or even an execution machine; the latter, as a matter of fact, is described as having a foundation deep in the earth and a working part (the writing part) suspended high up in the air. The burrow has, together with all these other literary creations of Kafka, the basic features of a metaphor, the method by which the writer imbues his text with several levels of meaning. Primarily, symbolic implications are the result of the extraordinary use of an everyday linguistic device; this consists of

[1] I am led to wonder whether it occurred to Kafka, who was interested in the linguistic implications of what he wrote and, in addition, fond of the pun, that the name Felice Bauer, so significant in his life, bears the import of "happy farmer."

[2] Some interpreters have surmised that the animal is a badger or a hamster; see Hermann Pongs, *Franz Kafka: Dichter des Labyrinths* (Heidelberg: Wolfgang Rothe, 1960), p. 385. Heinz Politzer, *Franz Kafka: Parable and Paradox* (Ithaca, N.Y.: Cornell University Press, 1962), proposes that it is "a mole rather than a badger" (p. 329). An alternative view of the animal's identity, namely that Kafka intended it to remain undisclosed, is proposed in my text.

comparing one object with another for convenience's sake. Thus, a chair "stands" on four "legs," and the driver of an automobile sits behind a "wheel." In literature the commonplace nature of such analogies is raised to the level of the artistic and, frequently, the esoteric. Established by Aristotle as a rhetorical device, used to produce an emphatic effect, the metaphor eventually became an essential feature in the realm of the written word. In literature the specificity or literalness of the image (so called by the literary critic I. A. Richards) in relation to the idea lying at the root of the comparison (called the tenor by Richards) loses its primacy; the sophistication of the interplay between image and tenor leads to the development of subcategories of metaphoric writing, such as the simile, personification, litotes, and the oxymoron. An example in medieval literature of the extent of the difference in metaphoric subtlety is afforded by the contrast between Wolfram von Eschenbach's use of the wound symbolism in *Parsifal* and Gottfried von Strassburg's rather elementary employment of the device of having the color of a ship's sail indicate whether or not Isolde is returning to the mortally wounded Tristan. In Kafka's case, the metaphors in his work are bold and almost overwhelming in their effect from the very beginning of his literary career. Kafka himself expressed his awareness of the possibilities inherent in the use of the metaphor when he examined both in his journal and in a letter to Felice Bauer the symbolic value of the figure of Georg Bendemann's friend in "Das Urteil." He proposed that the (nameless) character on whose veritable existence the story's plot rests represents in truth the relationship between father and son and the son's fiancée; the statements made by the narrator attesting to the friend's physical presence (in Russia) therefore are not to be taken literally. The adroitness with which Kafka invents further metaphors that become key factors in his fiction — the insect, the execution machine, the country doctor's patient, the humanized ape, among many more — increases geometrically in the course of Kafka's relatively brief period of creativity. Henry Sussman has indeed given his study of Kafka's work the title: *Franz Kafka: Geometrician of Metaphor* and has offered in his final chapter a critique of "the all-embracing metaphor," namely the burrow.

In a story written conceivably toward the end of 1914 Kafka himself sought, in my view, to illustrate the significance of the use of the metaphor in literature; at the same time he took some tentative steps in the direction of expressing his need to write in literary and philosophic (with just a suggestion of theologic) terms. The fragment "Der Riesenmaulwurf" ("The Giant Mole") as Brod, it is assumed, called it or "Der Dorfschullehrer" ("The Village Schoolteacher") as

Kafka referred to it concerns itself with a metaphor or a concept come to life.[3] The narrator, who, although he presents himself as an "I," is no longer the rebellious son of an authoritarian father, appears as a businessman (designated originally as an official, *Beamter*) who develops an obsession with the written word. The object of his passionate regard is a pamphlet published by an unknown or, rather, completely obscure village schoolmaster; it tells about the sighting in rural environs of a gigantic mole. A report of this phenomenon has reached the teacher, and he, despite the fact that he has not witnessed himself this appearance of the fanciful or fantastic in the real world, chooses to devote himself thereafter, most likely in his spare time, to the investigation of an intrusion of the extraordinary into the realm of the ordinary. (If he had been alive to write in the post-midcentury world, Kafka could possibly, but not very probably, have made symbolic use of a flying saucer sighting.) Since neither the protagonist, that is in this instance, the storyteller himself, nor his counterpart the schoolmaster, whom the narrator considers to be one of his opponents ("Gegner")[4] has personally ever seen the oversized mole, it necessarily remains for both an idea, a mental image; it has the dimensions of a simile in that it compares something in the natural world of vast proportions to an abstraction of overwhelming significance. In that light the huge mole can represent the hyperthropic nature of the literary endeavors undertaken by the two characters. When Kafka, considering his accomplishment in having completed "Das Urteil," proclaimed: "(An author) can only write *in this way*" ("Nur so kann geschrieben werden"), he expressed his sense of the vastness of the enterprise — his writing — in which he had become engaged. The metaphor of the giant mole makes apparent the magnification of the role he assigned his authorship to play in his life; the story itself analyzes the conflict between his goal as a writer and his goal as a young man to integrate himself in the community in which he lived.

At the outset the tale about the remarkable occurrence takes into account the fact that it was the common folk who, upon hearing from unknown sources about the unprecedented materialization, insisted that its significance must be probed. Kafka has his narrator specify: "Indeed, if several very plain people, people whose usual daily work didn't allow them to catch their breath in a moment of peace, if these

---

[3] See Wilhelm Emrich, *Franz Kafka* (Frankfurt am Main: Athenäum, 1960, II. ed.), p. 146.

[4] Franz Kafka, *Beschreibung eines Kampfes* (Frankfurt am Main: Fischer, 1976), p. 169. Further references to this book will appear in the text and/or end notes in parentheses with the rubric BK.

people hadn't taken up the cause (of delving into the mystery) unselfishly, the rumor of the apparition would scarcely have passed beyond the borders of the next county."[a] In this way, Kafka has, even before the turning point in his literary career, his vow to raise his fiction to the level of the pure, the true, the immutable, voiced his opinion that literature fulfills the needs of all humanity, especially of those who might seem to profit the least from it. Like the condemned man in "In der Strafkolonie" and all other previous victims of the execution machine they deserve to have knowledge, the truth, about the import of their lives.

The agency through which this revelation is to come to them, however, is in doubt. There are two portraits of the writer in the story, and the one contrasts with the other. The schoolmaster who writes the first critique of the phenomenon has a clear, if superficial resemblance to the author Kafka; the narrator (another quasi-double of Kafka) affords the teacher scant praise: "One left it to the old schoolteacher to adjudge the case, who was to be sure an excellent man in his field, but whose capabilities just as little as his education prepared him to produce a basic and furthermore creditable description (of the situation), let alone an explanation."[b] Kafka's intent in his early stories, e.g., in "Das Urteil," to provide a realistic description of his protagonist's problematic existence as well as a cogent explanation of it matches the goal which the storyteller sets for the schoolmaster in his pursuit of the truth about the mammoth mole. In his remarks about the study which the teacher subsequently published, the narrator might almost be commenting on a work such as "Das Urteil"; he proposes: "The small text was printed and sold in good numbers to the visitors to the village at that time; it also received some favorable attention, but the teacher was perceptive enough to recognize that his singular, entirely unsupported efforts were fundamentally worthless."[c] It needs to be mentioned again that Kafka never indicated that he aspired to write allegories and that therefore the premise that he referred directly in any one of his works to something he had previously published is at best speculative.[5] In addition to characteriz-

---

[5] Karlheinz Fingerhut in "Die Erzählungen," *Kafka Handbuch*, refers to "Der Riesen-maulwurf" in concurring with M.S. Pasley who maintains that Kafka's stories occasionally have cross-references: "M. S. Pasley's conclusion that Kafka had at times in his stories given thought to other of his stories can be confirmed at this point" ("M. S. Pasleys Ergebnis, Kafka habe zuweilen in Erzählungen über andere seiner Erzählungen nachgedacht, kann von hier aus bestätigt werden," p. 207). The crucial word in this interpretation, it seems to me, is "given thought to" ("nachgedacht"); pondering on other stories in one instance or several is to my mind not the same as making direct reference to them.

ing the schoolmaster's brochure about the giant mole in words that relate it to his own early efforts, Kafka portrays, through the narrator's reflections, the outsider figure's reservations about making his sparse work known to the general public. The storyteller expresses the view that the schoolmaster would actually prefer to keep his literary scribblings to himself and points to a postscript he has added to the pamphlet. The businessman, so fascinated by it, reports: "In this postscript he laments convincingly, perhaps less by way of skillfulness than by way of sincerity, the lack of understanding he has encountered from people from whom one would have least expected it."[d] This comment seems to come from the same source which had produced a litany of complaints from one whose God, whose family and especially whose father, also whose community had opposed his becoming a writer.

At this point in his explication of his relationship to the schoolmaster the narrator becomes expressly autobiographical; he confesses that, having initially not been concerned with the validity of the claim of the monstrous mole's reality made by the pedagogue, he had instead been intrigued by the opportunity to defend the writer's integrity (BK 168). The narrative in this instance clearly establishes the nature of the two characters it portrays and the nature of the confrontation which constitutes the story's plot. The businessman, it is apparent, in defending the tract's author, defends himself; the man from the city who is respected sets out to protect his inner and true self who is ridiculed for pretending both to be a writer and to have something significant to write about. In "In der Strafkolonie" Kafka undertakes much more vividly (critics have said all too vividly) and dramatically to analyze a similar situation. The world traveller and the businessman are both obliged to sit in judgment on a visionary living in a remote place in a kind of exile. In the one case the visitor to the penal colony attempts to remain impartial but is overwhelmed and then repulsed by the officer's ardency. The businessman, too, is taken aback by the vehemence with which the schoolteacher espouses his cause. "What did the defense of his honor mean to the teacher anyway!" he complains. "Only the cause, the cause concerned him at all."[e] The businessman-narrator's resentment aroused by the exclusivity of his counterpart's devotion to his work forces him to acknowledge the deficiency of his insight into his dedication to his own cause. He reaches this conclusion: "Such a giant mole is to be sure a wonder, but one may not expect the continuous attention of the world in regard to it, especially if the (very) existence of the mole has not been established beyond dispute and furthermore it can't be produced. And I have also admitted (to myself), I would probably never have stood up for the mole itself, if I had been its discoverer, in the same way that I have gladly and voluntarily stood up for the teacher."[f] In these words Kafka reveals his attitude toward the crisis which his life had engendered at the time when his attempt to combine writing with a career as a bureaucrat and concomitantly with marriage confronted him with the perils of a dichotomous existence. Facing symbolically the same problem, the enlightened visitor to the primitive penal colony runs away from an opportunity to support the visionary officer of the execution. Kafka made apparent his dissatisfaction with the irresolution evident in this ending both by confiding his discontent to his journal and by composing several versions (all incomplete) of an alternative ending. His indecision pervades the closing pages of "Der Dorfschullehrer."[6]

To the struggle between the irresolute businessman and the obscure but imaginative schoolmaster for the right to publish his findings about the interrelationship between the natural and the metaphysical worlds there is a witness keeping out of sight; as the narrator has explained there are those who actually saw the gigantic mole and spread abroad the news of its appearance. Therefore, it is of utmost importance to them not only that the phenomenon be explained to them but also that it be explained in terms that they can understand. The pedagogue tries in the last meeting between the two contenders to convince his scientifically, that is, rationalistically inclined opponent that as an intuitively oriented writer he is the better equipped craftsman and more devoted messenger to the people. He is, he says in the story's closing passages, responsible in the first instance to them, unlike the businessman who is responsible primarily to himself and/or the impersonal realm of science. Emrich provides a summary statement about the aftermath of this all but unending quarrel between two schools of thought; he maintains: "What remains is the sheer 'silent,' 'purposeless' existence of humanity.... It could speak of truth, which rises heaven-high over that which is (merely) reasonable."[7]

"Der Dorfschullehrer" marks a transitional phase in Kafka's writing. It poses the question which he was at this stage in his life still able to ask himself, whether or not he could forge a literary career for himself and at the same time achieve as an outsider the status of a

---

[6] Pascal in *Kafka's Narrators* is impelled to contend in regard to "Der Dorfschullehrer" or "Der Riesenmaulwurf": "This is truly an unfinished fragment" (p. 180).

[7] Emrich, *Franz Kafka*, p. 151. The quotation reads: "Was bleibt ist die pure 'stumme', 'zwecklose' Existenz des Menschen.... Diese stumme Existenz einzig weiß um die Erscheinung dieses Tieres. Sie könnte reden von der Wahrheit, die himmelhoch über jeden Verstand geht."

reputable member of society. He was, however, never required to provide an answer to the query posed by himself to himself. His illness put an end to his prospects of becoming both a family man and solid citizen and a writer of clear and perhaps vapid fiction (like Max Brod). In his article "Die Erzählungen" Karlheinz Fingerhut characterizes this phase of Kafka's development as a writer in regard to his use of symbolism by proposing: "The alienating outsider-existence symbolized by the giant mole is seen from a point of view outside the subject. The subject of *Metamorphosis* regarded from the subject's point of view is the object of the investigation and representation in *The Village Schoolmaster*."[8] Indicative of Kafka's having reached maturity in his ability to make full use of the metaphor, the symbol of the immaterial mole or mole-like being and his immense real structure the burrow is the great achievement of his last few stories.

Even in the face of the vast amount of descriptive passages devoted to the principal metaphor in "Die Verwandlung" or "In der Strafkolonie" or even "Josefine" (re: Josefine's singing), the attention paid to the burrow by the "I"-figure in the story, who created it, is phenomenal. Patently, the narrative consists of two parts, one in which the creature, the architect of the structure, lies just outside its entrance and relates it history and another in which the creative artist goes inside his "house," his habitation, and regards its soundness. (The animal's sexuality is not an issue in the narrative, but then its autobiographical import would suggest that the "I" is a he, rather than an "it.") His moving inside his burrow is the only bit of action which occurs in the tale's entirety, except for the coming into existence of the hissing he subsequently hears, which, in the final analysis, represents a perception, not an event. In choosing the format of an animal fable to depict the lot, that is, the experience, of the artist, Kafka deviated somewhat from his practice of using the form in order to reflect on the results of his decision to be a writer. Therefore, the identification of the protagonist with the characteristics of a specific animal is hardly a factor in "Der Bau"; in this way a theme such as Josefine's unmouse-like lack of diffidence (or the artist's perfectionism) does not occur as a subject for critical debate. Furthermore, the burrowing creature is, despite a passing reference to claws, not equipped by nature to dig. Rather, he makes his forehead into the tool with which he attacks hard earth or even solid rock. Thereby the significance of the metaphor

---

[8] Karlheinz Fingerhut, "Die Erzählungen," *Kafka Handbuch*, p. 286. The quotation reads: "Die befremdliche Sonderexistenz symbolisiert durch den Riesenmaulwurf, ist ganz von außen gesehen. Das perspektivtragende Subjekt der *Verwandlung* ist das Untersuchungs- und Darstellungsobjekt des *Dorfschullehrers*."

supersedes its meaningfulness as a comparison; the relationship between the mind and a digging instrument is a tenuous one at best. For Kafka, however, the image he wishes to convey lies close at hand, ready-made in a journal entry, dated November 5, 1911; it reads: "I want to write with a constant trembling (evident) on my forehead" ("Ich will schreiben, mit einem ständigen Zittern auf der Stirn"). The implication that the subject of "Der Bau" ("The Burrow/ Structure") is the analysis of a literary career and body of work is buttressed steadily by a series of metaphors which support one another. The burrow itself constitutes the keystone in the symbolic structure. It has an antithetical nature, consisting of substance — the earth — and shadow — the emptiness of its tunnels. The dichotomy of mind and body which is the fundament of philosophic thought finds expression in the portrayal of the creature's lying outside the entrance to his hidden realm with which the story begins. Interpreters of "Der Bau" have taken special note of the bifurcation which predominates in Kafka's imagery. Ingeborg Henel avers that Kafka has split the "I" of the narrator into a subject and an object, into the animal and his burrow.[9]

Critical consensus not only holds that Kafka intends the burrow to symbolize his work but also in the case of several proponents of this view undertakes to make it literal, that is, to identify the stories to which Kafka might be referring. It has been suggested that the section of the underground maze that lies just beyond the camouflaged opening would have to be Kafka's first true piece of fiction "Beschreibung eines Kampfes" or the "breakthrough" narrative "Das Urteil"; indeed the words "Urteil" (139) and "beurteile" (138) do occur in the text of "Der Bau." Since at the labyrinth's innermost point there lies a room labeled a citadel (*Burg*), the conclusion has been drawn that this final or ultimate construction represents *Das Schloß*, Kafka's last attempt to write a novel and his lengthiest work. The effort of some critics to emphasize the literalness of Kafka's metaphors and thus to devalue their multivalence seems to me to be derived from their conviction that his fiction can be better appreciated when read as allegory. This form of writing which considers a series of symbols to be links in a chain, parts of a whole that comes to light when they are properly assembled, must have a unifying element, symbolically called

---

[9] See Ingeborg Henel, "Periodisierung und Entwicklung" in *Kafka Handbuch II*, p. 238. Also concerned with the interplay of part and counterpart which characterizes the story, Hermann J. Weigand in his discussion of the narrative describes the course which it takes metaphorically as the tension created by the "two poles of an elliptical field of force," Hermann J. Weigand, "Franz Kafka's 'The Burrow' ('Der Bau'): An Analytical Essay," in *PMLA*, 87:2 (March 1972), p. 153.

a key, to unlock the mystery of their interrelationship. Accordingly, it is possible for the reader of "Die Verwandlung" to find that low or missing self-esteem has literally turned Gregor Samsa into a vermin and caused him under those circumstances to commit suicide. I would suggest, however, that, on the reader's part, taking the symbols to be open-ended and, by and large, unfathomable will provide a more satisfactory reading and, in addition, the occasion for a re-reading. The matter of which of his works are referred to in "Der Bau" is at best incidental. However, the presumption that the tenor of the maze is Kafka's analysis of his literary activities cannot be readily dismissed. The first-person narrator can but be the *author* Kafka who undertakes to regard his work from a critical perspective.[10] Once inside his creation, the creature necessarily loses his critical faculties since he has transformed himself into an abstraction, a metaphor, and for a brief time he experiences a paroxysm of contentment at the thought of his accomplishments. Like the hunger artist in heaven he feasts on the food for which he had no taste no earth. He plans to turn the castle keep, the *Burgplatz*, which lies at the center or in the heart of the maze into an eternally secure (mighty) fortress suspended in space like the sun — something immutable. But his moment of bliss is doomed to fade. In one of a series of paradoxical aphorisms which Kafka wrote, presumably in 1917-1918, and collected, numbering them in sequence, he apparently anticipated, at least philosophically, this turn of events. Number 69 proposes: "Theoretically, there is the possibility of (achieving) total happiness: (it depends on) believing in the immutable in one's self (and yet) not striving to achieve it."[11g]

At the beginning of the story the burrower errs in this regard: he contemplates the work that he has done and claims it to be a supreme achievement. He proposes: "I have put my burrow together, and it appears to be well-made."[h] The biblical undertone to these words is unmistakable: "And God saw every thing that he had made, and, behold, it was very good" (Genesis 1:31). The counterpart to this exultation follows immediately as a feature of Kafka's paradoxical treatment of his material. The wonderful world of the burrow has the

---

[10] In Heinrich Henel's study of "Der Bau" the argument is made that in addition to the voice of the narrator "the voice of the implied author (the person who is Kafka) is heard who ... adds a second perspective to that of the narrator-protagonist," H. Henel, "Kafka's *Der Bau* or How to Escape from a Maze" in *The Discontinuous Tradition*, ed. P. T. Ganz (Oxford: Clarendon Press, 1971), p. 230.

[11] Franz Kafka, *Hochzeitsvorbereitungen auf dem Lande* (Frankfurt am Main: Fischer, 1976), p. 35. Further references to this volume will appear in the text and/or end notes with the rubric H.

outward appearance of being a hole in the ground — nothing. But, so the creature contends, this supposed vacuum is actually something worth researching ("etwas Nachforschungswertes"). He goes on to explain that what appears to be the entrance to his maze is only a subterfuge on his part, a kind of lie, to conceal the fact that the real passageway starts elsewhere, not far away. Kafka thus begins his metaphoric portrayal of the lot of the artist/writer by contrasting the insubstantial but eternal realm of art with the real world, which is a world of appearances. The burrower's conviction that the creation which has sprung from his mind is in all respects superior to the real world lying just outside its entrance coincides with the theory put forward in another of Kafka's aphorisms that only the spiritual (insubstantial) world has permanence. Kafka maintains: "There is nothing else but a spiritual (mental) world; what we call the perceptible world is the evil in the spiritual, and what we call evil is only (the) inescapability of a moment in our everlasting development."[i] In this affirmation of a belief in the durability of that which transcends reality there lie concealed intimations of doubt; in its striving toward absolute purity, light necessarily casts a shadow, creates a flaw (evil) which may be slight and transitory but cannot be avoided. The great number of dualities, opposites — light and darkness, body and self, earth and air, etc. — which Kafka brings into play both in these opening pages of "Der Bau" and the sequence of aphorisms written earlier suggests that toward the end of his life Kafka markedly took an interest in the tenets of gnosticism. In this creed or philosophic system, the basic postulate envisions a rift in the nature of God or the absolute at the time of the creation of the universe; matter was separated from spirit, man from his maker or the source of his being. Out of the good, evil was born.

The perception of having made some fatal error in creating his burrow overwhelms the self-conscious animal even as he contemplates his almost completed work. "I live in the very heart of my house in peace, and in the meantime, slowly and silently, my adversary is boring his way through to me from some place or other," he laments.[j] The force which disturbs the peace of his sanctuary consists, as he proposes, not only of invaders from outside but also from internal but invisible destructive elements or faults. Kafka has anticipated the strife-ridden existence of the burrower in one of the collected aphorisms which bear the title, concocted by Brod, of "Observations concerning Sin, Suffering, Hope, and the True Way" ("Betrachtungen über Sünde, Leid, Hoffnung und den wahren Weg").[12] Number 66 pictures the conflicted existence of the human animal: "He is a free and secure citizen of the earth, for he is bound on a chain (or leash) which is long enough to give him free reign (to enter) all earthly rooms, and yet only long enough so that nothing can compel him (to go) beyond the borders of the earth. At the same time he is, however, a free and secure citizen of heaven, for he is also bound on a similarly functioning heavenly chain. If he wants to reach the earth, the heavenly collar will choke him; if he wants to reach heaven, the earthly one (will do the same). And yet in spite of everything all possibilities are open to him — this he feels; indeed, he even refuses to put the blame for the entire affair on a mistake (made) on the occasion of the initial enchainment."[k] (Even though these philosophic passages are not as replete with metaphors as the stories are, there are instances, such as this one, where an image prominent in the fiction — here it is the human being in the guise of a lowly dog — is reintroduced.) Placed midway between earthly time and eternity, humankind, as Kafka envisions its destiny, knows death without having the assurance that the God-given self is immortal.

Kafka suggests that this same situation exists in the biblical myth of the expulsion from the Garden of Eden; in another of the aphorisms he provides an exegesis of the event at the beginning of time. The expulsion, he maintains, is irredeemable in two senses — Adam and Eve were excluded from being in paradise (in God's presence) in eternity and in time were continually being driven out. Yet, paradoxically, the sum of these two minuses is a plus, since the possibility thus exists that all of humanity, in the stead of the first man and woman, have never left the garden: "The everlasting nature of the occurrence ... makes it possible, nevertheless, that we might indeed not only stay in paradise, but that we actually continue to be there, whether we know it or not."[l] The ramifications of this dilemma are those which confront the animal in his burrow. He has constructed his own sphere of eternity, his paradise, a maze of the mind, but it is anchored in the earth and therefore is transient, as he is despite the shelter that he has built.

As the animal lies outside his underground maze and gives voice to his fear that there is a flaw in his concept of paradise, he tries to reassure himself by counting the satisfactions he can enjoy in his subterranean heaven. "The best thing about my construction is above

---

[12] It must remain a matter of conjecture whether or not Brod intentionally connected, by the use of "Betrachtung(en)," this late work with *Betrachtung*, Kafka's first published book.

all the silence," he muses.[m] Here Kafka once more and most pointedly makes use of the image of inaudible or almost inaudible music —
the kind with which he had already associated the dancing dogs and
Josefine's singing. In a reworking of the myth of Ulysses and the
Sirens, Kafka provides further insight into the overwhelming nature of
pure silence, the silence of God, the silence of the universe. He pictures
the Sirens as uttering the deadliest of sounds — no sound at all. Unlike
Ulysses who puts wax in his ears so that he will not have to succumb
to the lure of listening to the sound of immortality and dying in
ecstasy, Kafka's literary recreation of the figure wants to revel in the
purity of the void in the voices of the Sirens. What the burrower hears
is the silence of words on a page, but wills it to be pure silence. In his
essay on "Der Bau," H. Henel regards the symbol of silence as having
quite another implication. "Silence and emptiness are what frighten
(the animal)," he contends.[13] Henel reaches this conclusion on basis
of the premise that the construction undertaken by the burrower
represents an attempt to escape life, to hide himself away in something
resembling a tomb — "the realm of death — silent, mute, and
hollow."[14] However, the animal-architect of the maze not only yearns
for silence, he also associates it with another kind of bliss, the bliss of
sleep. "There I sleep the sweet sleep of peacefulness, of assuaged
longing, of having reached the goal of possessing a home," he
professes.[n] Since the burrower contrasts the peace within his tunnels
with the restlessness which plagues most of earth's wanderers or those
who live in packs, "delivered up to all the ruinations of heaven and
earth" ("ausgeliefert allem Verderben des Himmels und der Erde"), the
supposition that he has dug his maze in order to punish himself for his
self-centered way of life is, in my opinion, if not a misreading of the
text, then a matter of overemphasizing a minor theme in the work.[15]

---

[13] H. Henel, "Kafka's *Der Bau*," p. 227.

[14] Ibid., p. 233.

[15] In Bert Nagel's *Franz Kafka*, "Der Bau" is interpreted on this basis: "Kafka's central
theme of guilt, judgment and punishment thus is also — *expressis verbis* — basic in
this story" (p. 291). The quotation reads: "Kafkas zentrale Thematik von Schuld,
Gericht und Strafe liegt also — *expressis verbis* — auch dieser Erzählung zugrunde."
Reading the narrative in this light leads Nagel to put great emphasis on the
burrower's vanity and to reach this to my mind rather restrictive conclusion: "The
aesthete, who only acted out his life (as a vehicle for) vain self-satisfaction, falls
victim to the pitiless moralist (in Kafka) in the end" (p. 315) ("Der Ästhet, der in
eitlem Selbstgenuß sein Leben nur spielte, fällt zum Schluß dem gnadenlosen
Moralisten zum Opfer").

In the first part of the story, the protagonist and narrator deals with the problem of his being self-absorbed and too little involved in mundane matters, e.g., making a living, which appears here in the metaphor of hunting (cf. the hunting dog in "Forschungen"). He excuses himself for the excessive attention he pays the burrow ("Zuviel beschäftigt mich der Bau") on the grounds that he was not destined to find practical solutions to the enigmas with which he was confronted. "In addition," he avows, "I am not destined for and subjected to (living) a (naturally) free life, but I know that my days are numbered, that I am not compelled to hunt here more endlessly, but that in a figurative way when I am ready and tired of life here (on earth) someone will call me to him, whose invitation I will not be able to refuse."[o] Nevertheless, the burrower, as convinced as he is that it has been his mission to create the maze and let himself be absorbed by it, resists to the last making the ultimate commitment to his life's work, to disappear into it completely, to become *der Verschollene*. He rehearses once again all the arguments for taking this irreversible action, insisting, for example, that living in the silence and solitude of his lair ("Und alles, alles still und leer") will result in perfect bliss. Reassured, he gives up lying in wait to attack the "destroyer," who he anticipates is lurking in the world outside his burrow, and descends into the region of his work. In other words, he becomes literature; he has transformed himself not into something physically present like the vermin but into nothing, an abstraction, a metaphor.

The pattern evolved in the first part of "Der Bau" is repeated in the second; the initially positive point of view of the burrower is undermined in slow stages. Having entered the realm of timelessness ("always within my structure I have endless time" / "immer innerhalb des Baues habe ich endlose Zeit"), the protagonist solemnly reaffirms the purposes of his mission. He announces: "For your sake, you pathways and open places, and for your questions above all, (you) citadel, I have come indeed, (and) have held my life to be worthless (nothing)."[P] Comforted by the silence and the emptiness of the maze, the animal falls into a deep sleep. At this point, while he is defenseless, his pursuer, the doubts about his calling which he has brought with him into his lair like an infection, make their presence felt or, better, heard. The burrower is awakened by the sound of a faint hissing. A symbol almost as complex as that of the burrow itself, the inarticulate noise that eventually floods the tunnels and threatens to drown their occupant has been interpreted in numerous ways. In accord with the expectation that Kafka's metaphors will have a literal or realistic aspect, H. Henel contends that the hissing "may be his breath, panting from all the running around and digging," then adds in a coda "but

in a deeper sense it is his fear of the void."[16] Mark Boulby in his
study of the story gives the symbol a biographical significance, labeling
it "Kafka's fantasy about his own breathing, as his condition worsens
in the advanced stages of tuberculosis."[17] The first, rather casual
assumption made by the narrator that what he hears is the scampering
around of tiny creatures on the periphery of his labyrinth leads him,
as Sussman has pointed out, to treat the situation almost as if it were
a writing assignment: "The noise is described," Sussman avers, "as an
entry in an etymological dictionary, whose derivation (*Herkunft*...) must
be determined."[18] Becoming aware that he is overly preoccupied
with the omnipresent hissing sound, the burrower decides to reassure
himself of its insignificance; he becomes an interpreter of his story
himself and explains: "My own blood is (just) drumming much too
much in my ear...." ("Allzusehr klopft das eigene Blut im Ohr....").
Weaving his way through a maze of metaphors, the burrow's
inhabitant even associates the noise with the very silence for the sake
of which he had built his own lair: "It is as if the wellspring were
opening from which the silence of the burrow pours forth."[q] This
indulging himself in a feast of metaphoric language and literary
references has been a feature of the creature's existence in the burrow,
and even when he was on the point of entering his hideaway, the
narrator had sought to wound himself verbally by depicting his
hurling himself into a thorn bush. The punishment he inflicted on
himself in this fashion was called for because of his blasphemous or at
least egocentric appropriation of a biblical myth to represent his own
situation. The appearance of God in the burning bush to spur Moses
on in carrying out his mission lies at the root of this episode. The
convolutions of the metaphoric sphere of "Der Bau" — the protagonist
even envisions separating the *Burgplatz*, the mind or the brain, from
the body, the rest of the structure — are maddeningly intricate; Kafka
has even borrowed the symbol of the hissing sound from his own
story "Die Verwandlung." In it the insect, venturing for the first time
to set foot outside his room in his altered state, is driven back into
hiding by his mighty opponent, his father, who cannot speak in his
rage but hisses.

The progress Kafka has made in his endeavor to raise his work to
the level of the pure, true and immutable can be measured by the fact

---

[16] H. Henel, "Kafka's *Der Bau*", p. 227.

[17] Mark Boulby, "Kafka's End: A Reassessment of 'The Burrow,'" *The German Quarterly*, 55:2 (March 1982), 184.

[18] Sussman, *Franz Kafka, Geometrician of Metaphor*, p. 151.

that the autobiographical element in his fiction, represented by the father figure as the opponent, the force with which the protagonist must contend, has been transmuted into an abstraction in "Der Bau." The metaphors Kafka employs in the last stage of his literary career have lost much of their literalness and gained in return greater sophistication. The depth of their meaning has been vastly increased; Kafka's forehead, his *Stampfhammer* (BK 137) (roughly, "pile-driver"), has fashioned images with a wide range of significance. The hissing also acquires a mythological dimension; in connection with the simulation in "Der Bau" of the story of the expulsion from the Garden of Eden and the fall of human beings from their state of innocence and living in eternity, the hissing heard by the burrower can but suggest the presence of the snake, the destroyer, in paradise. In the "Betrachtungen" ("Observations") Kafka discusses in the terse form of the maxim not only the meaning of the concept of an earthly paradise but also the concept of the fall, the expulsion from Eden. He seeks to shed new light on the latter event. "Why do we lament over the fall (from grace)?" he asks. "Not because of it have we been expelled from paradise, but because of the tree of life so that we might not eat of it. We are not sinful only because we have eaten of the tree of knowledge, but also because we have not yet eaten of the tree of life. Sinful is the state in which we find ourselves, regardless of (our) guilt."[T] In keeping with these tenets of a philosophy of life, Kafka replaces, referring to the digging creature and his writer-self, the stigma of the outsider engaged in a self-aggrandizing activity with the stigma of the flawed human being, incapable of widening the horizons of his life — of searching for truth. In the person of the narrator, Kafka forces himself to acknowledge the inevitability of the expulsion from paradise, the inadequacy of the burrow, his work, as a bulwark against the attack of the agents of mortality, human failure mentally and physically. Once again, one of Kafka's "observations" or maxims lends itself readily to use as a tool with which to grasp the implications of the closing pages of "Der Bau." Number 86 deals with the difference between the kind of knowledge afforded humanity by a bite into the apple (probably a pomegranate) and the kind of knowledge which would have been afforded humanity had they dared to taste the fruit of the tree of life. In the first instance, the knowledge gained has limited applicability; it pertains to the world of things, the chief characteristic of which is its temporality. (Kafka frequently employs the symbol of the clock to depict this functional and yet restricted and restricting kind of thinking.) The broader kind of knowledge, only approximately defined as wisdom, has the quality of the absolute, the truth.

The protagonist in "Der Bau" comes to realize that he is living in exile from paradise even in his burrow; he seeks to deal with the hissing sound in the limited light shed on his situation by human knowledgeability, that is, the extent to which human beings in their mortality can assess their own fallibility or culpability. A captive in his own castle keep, the burrower is compelled to draw two dismal conclusions. First, in his role as a representative of the writer Kafka, contemplating his reliance on the durability of his work, he must confront its impermanence and inadequacy. Kafka's fifty-seventh aphorism pictures this situation: "Language (words) can only be used (to represent) everything outside of the physical world only figuratively, but never even approaching comparatively (that is, literally or referentially), since it (language) in correspondence with (that is, as a part of) the physical world can only deal with possession and its ramifications."[5] In this respect, Kafka, in bringing his story to a close, confronts the possibility that his attempt to express the pure, the true, the immutable in his work has been doomed from the start. The other conclusion the being in the maze must reach in considering the significance of the hissing sound is that his structure and, indeed, no earthly structure at all can withstand physical decay, that is, its mortality. A number of commentators have associated the hissing with the approach of death and have taken it to be a literal representation of Kafka's fatal illness; he was dying of the effects of tuberculosis. It had in running its course damaged and then destroyed his larynx so that in his last days he could not speak. It is a matter of the ultimate kind of irony that the writer who figuratively gave up his life to write died when he was capable of communicating only by writing. The being he had aspired to be mentally, an inhabitant of Eden with access to the tree of life and its fruit, providing insight into the truth about himself and his life, he was now being compelled to surrender, because his physical self which he had excoriated, starved, twisted into every grim shape imaginable, at last could avenge itself.

In a long letter analyzing his writing career written to Max Brod on July 5, 1922, Kafka foresaw the end that it would take. "What the naive person sometimes wishes for himself: 'I would like to die and see how they mourn me,' this such a writer as I am experiences continually.... The reasons for fearing death can be divided into two main categories. First of all, he is terribly afraid of death because he has not yet (actually) lived.... The second main category ... is the contemplation: 'What I have only acted out, will now really happen to me. All my life I have been dying, and now I will truly die.... I have not bribed my way (out of death) by writing.'"[19t] In "Der Bau" Kafka has left or been forced to leave unanswered the question of whether or not it is indeed death that stalks the defenseless burrower. The manuscript of the story has no ending; several critics have concluded that only a few sentences would be required to bring it to a close. One of the interpreters Hermann Weigand, convinced that this is surely the case, has provided the missing ending. He eliminates the deadly confrontation with the animal's ever-present adversary, a feature of several other projections of what a final paragraph or two would contain, and supposes instead that the animal would have died quietly in his sleep.[20] Treating the problem of an ending with greater subtlety, Stanley Corngold proposes: "Kafka projects for writer and reader an unawed consciousness of death."[21] But in the narrative's concluding pages Kafka himself afforded a clue about the missing ending or, better, the lack of an ending. In describing his confusion as to whether or not his opponent is an enemy or the second self he has created, he makes the assertion that he would rather not know. He begins: "This trench (*Graben* which is a cognate of "grave") is to afford me certainty? I have reached the stage of not even wanting to have certainty."[u] He has reached the point at which he despairs of finding answers and of resolving the riddle of the series of antitheses his life has evolved. The certainty that he refused to face in regard to himself (and no one can blame him) was twofold. First of all, the truth in all its physical substantiality was that he was going to die as a young man, scarcely over forty years of age, never having had his own home and family and never having achieved appreciable recognition for his contribution to the art of literature to which he had devoted his life. In the matter of the sparseness of his published work and the vast amount of writing he had done only to be read by a few friends, Kafka could not have wanted to face the possibility that it fell far short of the goal that he had set for it and himself. One of his "Betrachtungen" ("Observations") reaches this bitter conclusion: "Our art consists of being blinded by the truth: The light upon the retreating gargoyle face is true, but nothing else (is)."[v]

[19] Kafka, *Briefe 1902-1924*, p. 384 f.

[20] Weigand, "'Der Bau,'" p. 164.

[21] Stanley Corngold, *Franz Kafka: The Necessity of Form* (Ithaca & London: Cornell University Press, 1988), p. 285.

Notes

a. "Ja, hätten nicht einzelne ganz einfache Leute, deren gewöhnliche Tagesarbeit ihnen kaum ein ruhiges Aufatmen gestattete, hätten nicht diese Leute uneigennützig sich der Sache angenommen, das Gerücht von der Erscheinung wäre wahrscheinlich kaum über den nächsten Umkreis hinausgekommen" (BK 166).

b. "(Man) überließ die einzige schriftliche Behandlung des Falls dem alten Dorflehrer, der zwar ein ausgezeichneter Mann in seinem Berufe war, aber dessen Fähigkeiten ebensowenig wie seine Vorbildung es ihm ermöglichte, eine gründliche und weiterhin verwertbare Beschreibung, geschweige denn eine Erklärung zu liefern" (BK 166).

c. "Die kleine Schrift wurde gedruckt und an die damaligen Besucher des Dorfes viel verkauft, sie fand auch einige Anerkennung, aber der Lehrer war klug genug einzusehen, daß seine vereinzelten, von niemandem unterstützten Bemühungen im Grunde wertlos waren" (BK 167).

d. "In diesem Nachtrag führt er, vielleicht nicht durch Geschicklichkeit, aber durch Ehrlichkeit über die Verständnislosigkeit, die ihm bei Leuten begegnet ist, wo man sie am wenigsten hätte erwarten sollen" (BK 167).

e. "Was bedeutete denn für den Lehrer die Verteidigung seiner Ehrenhaftigkeit! An der Sache, nur an der Sache lag ihm" (BK 171).

f. "Ein so großer Maulwurf ist gewiß eine Merkwürdigkeit, aber die dauernde Aufmerksamkeit der ganzen Welt darf man nicht dafür verlangen, besonders wenn die Existenz des Maulwurfs nicht vollständig einwandfrei festgestellt ist und man ihn jedenfalls nicht vorführen kann. Und ich gestand auch ein, daß ich mich wahrscheinlich für den Maulwurf selbst, wenn ich der Entdecker gewesen wäre, niemals so eingesetzt hätte, wie ich es für den Lehrer gern und freiwillig tat" (BK 171).

g. "Theoretisch gibt es eine vollkommene Glücksmöglichkeit: An das Unzerstörbare in sich glauben und nicht zu ihm streben."

h. "Ich habe den Bau eingerichtet und er scheint wohlgelungen" (BK 132).

i. "Es gibt nichts anderes als eine geistige Welt; was wir sinnliche Welt nennen, ist das Böse in der geistige Welt; was wir sinnliche Welt nennen, ist das Böse in der geistigen, und was wir böse nennen, ist nur eine Notwendigkeit eines Augenblicks unserer ewigen Entwicklung" (BK 34).

j. "Ich lebe im Innersten meines Hauses in Frieden und inzwischen bohrt sich langsam und still der Gegner von irgendwoher an mich heran" (BK 133).

k. "Er ist ein freier und gesicherter Bürger der Erde, denn er ist an eine Kette gelegt, die lang genug ist, um ihm alle irdischen Räume frei zu geben, und doch nur so lang, daß nichts ihn über die Grenzen der Erden reißen kann. Gleichzeitig aber ist er auch ein freier und gesicherter Bürger des Himmels, denn er ist auch an eine ähnliche berechnete Himmelskette gelegt. Will er nun auf die Erde, drosselt ihn das Halsband des Himmels, will er in den Himmel, jenes der Erde. Und trotzdem hat er alle Möglichkeiten und fühlt es; ja, er weigert sich sogar, das Ganze auf einen Fehler bei der ersten Fesslung zurückzuführen" (BK 35).

l. "Die Ewigkeit des Vorganges ... macht es trotzdem möglich, daß wir nicht nur dauernd im Paradiese bleiben könnten, sondern tatsächlich dort dauernd sind, gleichgültig ob wir es hier wissen oder nicht" (Nos. 64/65, H 35).

m. "Das Schönste an meinem Bau ist aber die Stille" (BK 134).

n. "Dort schlafe ich den süßen Schlaf des Friedens, des beruhigten Verlangens, des erreichten Zieles des Hausbesitzes" (BK 134).

o. "Auch bin ich nicht dem freien Leben bestimmt und ausgeliefert, sondern ich weiß, daß meine Zeit gemessen ist, daß ich nicht endloser hier jagen muß, sondern daß mich gewissermaßen, wenn ich will und des Lebens hier müde bin, jemand zu sich rufen wird, dessen Einladung ich nicht werde widerstehen können" (BK 140).

p. "Euretwegen, ihr Gänge und Plätze und deine Fragen vor allem, Burgplatz, bin ich ja gekommen, habe mein Leben für nichts geachtet...." (BK 149).

q. "Es ist, als öffne sich die Quelle, aus welcher die Stille des Baues strömt" (BK 157).

r. "Warum klagen wir wegen des Sündenfalls? Nicht seinetwegen sind wir aus dem Paradiese vertrieben worden, sondern wegen des Baumes des Lebens, damit wir nicht von ihm essen. Wir sind nicht nur deshalb sündig, weil wir vom Baum der Erkenntnis gegessen haben, sondern auch deshalb, weil wir vom Baum des Lebens noch nicht gegessen haben. Sündig ist der Stand, in dem wir uns befinden, unabhängig von Schuld" (H 36 f.).

s. "Die Sprache kann für alles außerhalb der sinnlichen Welt nur andeutungsweise, aber niemals auch nur annähernd vergleichsweise gebraucht werden, da sie, entsprechend der sinnlichen Welt nur vom Besitz und seine Beziehungen handelt" (H 34).

t. "Was der naive Mensch sich manchmal wünscht, 'Ich wollte sterben und sehn, wie man mich beweint,' das verwirklicht ein solcher Schriftsteller (wie ich es bin) fortwährend.... Die Gründe für die Todesangst lassen sich in zwei Hauptgruppen teilen. Erstens hat er schreckliche Angst zu sterben, weil er noch nicht gelebt hat.... Der zweite Hauptgrund ... ist die Überlegung: 'Was ich gespielt habe, wird wirklich geschehen. Mein Leben lang bin ich gestorben und nun werde ich wirklich sterben.... Ich habe mich durch das Schreiben nicht losgekauft."

u. "Dieser Graben soll mir Gewißheit bringen? Ich bin so weit, daß ich Gewißheit gar nicht haben will" (BK 163).

v. "Unsere Kunst ist ein von der Wahrheit Geblendet-Sein: Das Licht auf dem zurückweichenden Fratzengesicht ist wahr, sonst nichts" (H 35).

Conclusion

An Inroad on the Last Frontier

WHEN KAFKA EARLY in his youth began to write as a literary activity, he immediately experienced what he considered to be the opposition of inner and outer forces in his world. His complaint to his one close friend at the time that God stood in the way of his becoming a writer indicates his awareness that there was a self-critical, self-destructive element in his being which lay at the root of his need to reflect on life rather than participate in it. A more readily perceived kind of disapproval was also his father's discontent, expressed unmistakably, with a son who was apparently growing up to follow in the footsteps of the intellectually inclined men in his wife's family. In addition, it happened that when Franz undertook on the occasion of a family gathering to let others read what he had written in private, the relative to whom he gave this example of his literary efforts soon handed it back while commenting to those around him: "The usual stuff." Inevitably then, the theme of the conflict between the compulsion to give expression to the self in artistic, that is, non-utilitarian activity and the need to pursue pragmatic, socially acceptable goals became one of the principal features in Kafka's literary work.

In the course of his career as a writer he sought by means of various metaphors to describe the purpose that writing imaginative literature (fiction) served. Initially, he regarded a literary work as a tool to be used in exploring the self; in a letter to Oskar Pollak he proposes: "Many a book acts as a key to the unknown (foreign) rooms in our own castle."[1] Besides providing a link to the concepts which he would explore in *Das Schloß*, the last of his three unfinished novels, the metaphoric definition Kafka evolved in this early stage of his literary ventures places emphasis on the exploration of the self as the goal to be obtained. A duplicate of this assessment with an even more striking metaphor occurs in a subsequent letter: "A book must be the axe for (to break open) the frozen sea in us."[2] The several versions of

---

[1] Kafka, *Briefe 1902-1924*, p. 20. The quotation reads: "Manches Buch wirkt wie ein Schlüssel zu fremden Sälen des eignen Schlosses."

[2] Ibid., p. 28. "Ein Buch muß die Axt sein für das gefrorene Meer in uns."

Kafka's story "Beschreibung eines Kampfes" ("Description of a Struggle") attest to the intensity of his effort at the beginning of his career as a writer to portray the multiplicity of selves or the amorphous character of the self which lay concealed in the physical presence which was Franz Kafka. The antithetical nature of these two entities, the outward and inward person, is an important property of this early piece of prose, destined to recur in a multiplicity of much more sophisticated forms in all his fiction. A dramatically terse example of the reappearance of this theme in Kafka's work can be found in one of the prose sketches which comprise the content of his first publication in book form *Betrachtung* (*Meditation*, but, better, *Observation*). "Wunsch, Indianer zu werden" consists of this single sentence: "If only one were an Indian, and thus prepared (equipped), and on the galloping horse, aslant the air, would for an instant continue to tremble above the trembling earth, until one left his spurs, for there were (no longer) any spurs, until one cast off the reins, for there were (no longer) any reins, and (until one) scarcely saw the ground ahead like a level mowed-down meadow, (without seeing even) the horse's neck and head."[a] Here the separation of the mental self from the physical self is metaphorically pictured as a dream or fantasy. This depiction is a prelude to the extensive treatment of the same bifurcation which is symbolized much more subtly and at much greater length in "Der Bau" by the burrower (the material self) and the burrow (the immaterial self).

Kafka soon began to give his study of the dichotomous self a familial background in order to provide a greater degree of objectivity to his analysis of his outsiderness, his quarrel with social norms. In a sense, "Wunsch, Indianer zu werden" deals with a search on the artist's (writer's) part for freedom from the tensions created by his conflict with society; the latter subject patently undergoes a definitive scrutiny in Kafka's last story, "Josefine." The figure representing the counterpart to the nonconformist (the drunkard in "Beschreibung eines Kampfes," the fantasizing author of "Wunsch, Indianer zu werden," etc.) first appears in the only true narrative in *Betrachtung*, "Unglücklichsein" ("In a State of Misery"). In it Kafka tells of the encounter between an unhappy young man who has evoked a ghost or a ghost-self in his room and a fellow boarder whom he happens to encounter on the stairs. The latter seeks without ill will to put an end to his neighbor's belief in ghosts. "You can never get a clear answer (bit of information) from them.... These ghosts seem to be more dubious about their existence than we are about ours...."[b] Converting this chance meeting into the psychologically profound struggle between father and son, the agony of which he knew personally, Kafka wrote what he considered to be his breakthrough story, his first impressive work of fiction — "Das Urteil" ("The Judgment" or "The Sentence"). Taking the tale to be the kind of achievement which justified the sacrifice his devotion to the cause of enlightenment through literature demanded, he hailed it as a victory in his journal: "*Only in this way* can one write, only with such cohesion, with such complete baring of the body and the soul."[3c] Kafka's attempt to duplicate the success he felt he had achieved with "Das Urteil" by producing a lengthier and even more striking story, once again based on the theme of self-revelation, "Die Verwandlung" ("Metamorphosis" or "The Transformation"), gave him some satisfaction but, because he encountered difficulties in bringing it to a close, made him aware of the limitations this kind of writing inherently entailed. The goal he seems to have set for himself of exposing an inner conflict in his fiction began to be regarded as too limited an objective. In a letter to Max Brod written in 1913 he revealed his dissatisfaction with the role he was playing as an author. He protested: "Images such as this one, in which I am lying stretched out on the floor, carved up like a roast, and am slowly pushing with my hand a slice of the meat toward a dog (waiting) in the corner — these kinds of image are meals for my head every day."[4d]

The repulsiveness which characterizes Kafka's portrayal of his plight as an author recurs in his story "In der Strafkolonie" ("In the Penal Colony") which analyzes the situation in an expanded and decidedly more profound fashion. The narrative's outstanding feature in regard to Kafka's development as a writer is the widening of its horizons; it does not take place in the narrow confines of an inner-city apartment, nor is its protagonist a hopelessly downtrodden servant of European bureaucracy. A scientist on an exploratory trip around the world (not unlike Darwin) is now the focal point of the narrator's interest. This representative of an enlightened and technologically sophisticated civilization finds himself by chance in a remote corner of the world in the midst of a still primitive society. Invited to witness a public execution (all members of the community are convicts, having been born guilty), the world traveller meets his counterpart in the person of the officer in charge of carrying out the death sentence; the

---

[3] Franz Kafka, *Tagebücher 1910-1923* (Frankfurt am Main: Fischer, 1976), p. 214.

[4] Kafka, *Briefe 1902-1924*, p. 114 f.

fanatic, the madman here confronts the man of science, of reason.[5]
They stand together in the presence of the Word made manifest, a
printing machine which is also an execution machine. Somewhat like
the man who might be an author pictured by Kafka as feeding himself
to the dog, the officer in the penal colony feeds himself to the machine
in order to convince the recalcitrant witness that martyrdom (the
writer's giving up of his life in the world) is the reward granted those
who serve society by dedicating themselves to the exploration of the
self in a search for truth (self-knowledge). When the officer's body is
mangled on the deadly instrument and spewed from it, the visitor
turns his back on the phantasmagoric pageant and runs away. The
imagery in this scene depicts Kafka's flight from the obligation he had
placed on himself to be unsparing in the self-examination which he
was convinced was the entire purpose of the art of creative writing.
However, the disavowal of this premise with which "In der
Strafkolonie" closes or seems to close left Kafka dissatisfied, and he
sought to find yet other endings. These failed efforts to bring to a
resolution the conflict between the demands made upon him by society
and his need to write appear in his journal for the year 1917 in which
Kafka declares his enthusiasm for "Ein Landarzt" and sets for himself
the goal of achieving the pure, the true, the immutable in his writing.

A number of events in his life have enabled him to put aside his
reservations about the necessity of devoting himself exclusively to his
literary pursuits. His succumbing to a tubercular infection was, as he
put it, a matter of his body's avenging the neglect it had endured on
the part of his intellect. His illness had predictably monumental
consequences: a forced retirement from his debilitating office work, an
end to his recurring engagement to Felice Bauer, for which there was
now no purpose at all, and, as a consequence of these motive forces
(Kafka would call them "motivations"), the occasion to "research" the
nature of writing and the writer particularly in relation to their social
significance. "Ein Landarzt" marks the beginning of this pilgrimage to
the source of the truth which literature seeks to mirror rather than the
perceived world, the world of surfaces and appearances, "lies," as
Kafka now held.

The protagonist in "Ein Landarzt" is like the researcher in "In der
Strafkolonie" a man of science, a physician. But he leads a
dream-haunted life; from this realm of the subconscious he receives a

---

[5] Shimon Sandbank in *After Kafka* has reached an apt conclusion about the function
of the symbolism in "In der Strafkolonie": "This embedding (of the fantastic in the
ordinary) produces in Kafka the effect of the Freudian 'uncanny,' the appearance of
archaic, primary thinking in the conscious, wide awake mind" (p. 130).

call and without much hesitation pursues it, entering into the insubstantial world of metaphor. His destiny becomes intertwined with that
of his patient, his writer-self, who bears the stigmata of the outsider —
mentally a wish to die and physically a gruesome and fatal wound
below the waist. The people of the community in which the
patient-artist lives celebrate the physician's healing arts and initiate
him into their society. But their expectations are not met: the patient
(the writer-self) dies, the doctor having failed him. In chagrin the latter
flees, intent on returning to the safe world of rationality, but reaches
only its border, the land of limbo, where he remains as a symbol of the
eternal outsider: "Naked, exposed to the freezing cold of this most
unfortunate of times, with an earthly carriage (and) unearthly horses,
I, old man that I am, circle aimlessly around."[e] In another narrative
from the *Ein Landarzt* collection, "Ein Bericht für eine Akademie"
Kafka issues another and equally negative report on the subject of a
being from the primitive world, here the natural rather than the dream
world, who hides his outsiderness behind a mask of conformity and
is just as miserable as the forlorn country doctor. The outsider figure
in the four stories in *Ein Hungerkünstler*, published in the last year of
Kafka's life, and also in "Forschungen eines Hundes" (left in manuscript form) concerns himself with himself or, in one case, herself in
the situation of the committed artist. In this way the tension or conflict
which constitutes the plot in Kafka's fiction emerges between the
incommensurability of the artist's mission and the simple needs of the
people which his or her work is meant to meet. In "Ein Landarzt"
there was the mere suggestion that the healing which the doctor was
being asked to undertake might be more than medical in nature. The
protagonist resisted accepting the role of priest or minister, although
not in a religious sense, to the community. In "Erstes Leid," the first
of the four narratives, the artist-hero remains out of touch with his
audience; in fact, he avoids meeting their eyes. He devotes himself to
refining his art which consists of living in the upper air and devising
acrobatic acts (words and metaphors) to express the experience. In
"Eine kleine Frau" the view from above is changed to one at ground
level; the narrator-protagonist is depersonalized and takes the form of
the artist's sensitivity to criticism separated from the rest of him. The
little woman represents the questioning of the artist's motives by
society; casting suspicion on his high purposes causes the artist
unbearable anguish.

This feature in Kafka's delineation of the nature of the artist
becomes the center of attention in the title story, "Ein Hungerkünstler."
Its narrator also stresses the inequity between the amount of dedication
with which the artist imbues his work and the amount of notice the

public takes of his performance. Pertinent to an understanding of the depth of his devotion to his art is a consideration of the means he uses to express his sense of mission. His choice of fasting, eventually unto death, is evidence of his conviction that art can provide a quasi-religious experience. It should be noted that another of Kafka's metaphors with which he sought to define his writing compares it to prayer. What has taken place in the evolution of Kafka's thinking on the subject of writing fiction (literature) is a de-emphasis on the sociopsychological aspects of life in his work and a continually growing emphasis on the absolutes which provide life with its everlasting dimension, thus its continuity. Indeed the kind of truth that he sought to reveal in "Das Urteil" by dissecting the relationship between him and his father was a personal, specific truth, hardly applicable at the level of the pure, the true, the immutable. The truths of "Ein Hungerkünstler" and "Der Bau" are of another, higher order. In one of the eight notebooks containing literary sketches which Kafka left to be disposed of after his death he defined in metaphoric language the kind of art his literary efforts were intended to produce: "Art flies around truth, but with the definite intention not to get burned. Its genius consists of (the ability) to find a place in the dark of the void where the beam of light can be caught up powerfully, a place of which there had been no previous knowledge."[1] The hunger artist believes that his fasting will reflect perhaps just a glimmer of the pure light of the eternal. The sun is undoubtedly a universal symbol for the source not only of life itself but also of the consciousness which binds together human beings and thus of the source per se. It is, Kafka proposes, the artist's role to promulgate the message of this interrelationship by producing, in the writer's case, a text which in the purity of its design and the appropriateness (honesty) of its words will disclose the unmistakable truth. But the artist's fallibility, together with the remoteness of the community which he benefits and their impoverishment (physically and mentally), makes the fulfillment of his mission unlikely. Despite the hopelessness which dogs his footsteps Kafka in his last stories proceeds with his attempt to make an inroad on the last frontier, marking the border between the material and immaterial worlds. Werner Hoffmann has pictured this final stage in Kafka's thinking about the purport of his writing in this way: "(His 'entire work') was supposed to have become a new kabala, a new esoteric doctrine, which would have gone beyond earthly borders into a higher spiritual world."[6]

In two of his later stories Kafka specifically explored the relationship between the artist and his or her public. Both have been given the form of the animal fable and in that regard have a didactic tone suitable for the presentation of an argument or the statement of an opinion. "Forschungen eines Hundes" lets the voice of a humble dog be heard whose inquisitive mind compels him to go beyond the bounds of the obvious, beyond the borders of the everyday world. The subject he seeks to enlighten himself about is nourishment, food for the body, food for the mind. As he investigates the nature of the first, he becomes fascinated by the association it has with the second. To test the validity of the concept that edible food seems to spring up from the ground (the suggestion is that it has been planted), he declines to eat substances which lie on the ground. Finding that food of this kind will occasionally be hurled down from above, he hides himself away in order to make the source which plants in this strange fashion reveal itself. In his seclusion he ponders over a related matter, the phenomenon of the dancing dogs who engage in the unusual practice of distancing themselves from the earth (where their food lies) in order to prance about on their hind legs. The possibility that they produce ethereal music, or seem to, that accompanies their unfitting behavior intrigues the four-legged scientist, but his attempt to approach the performers is thwarted. Still their appearance has reminded the researcher of another matter, the debatable existence of up-in-the-air dogs, a legendary breed. No rational explanation for their antics occurs to the enquiring dog although it strikes him that they, too, have the capacity to evoke musical sounds out of the air and therefore have a somewhat uncertain relationship to dogs that walk upright. The conclusion which readers of "Forschungen eines Hundes" are apt to reach, although the researcher only has an inkling of it, is that the out-of-the-ordinary canines are artists, in part performing a service, in part expressing their idiosyncrasies (the word *Luftmensch* is cant for a daydreamer). As a result of the negative impact of his experimentation on himself, the dog is close to dying of starvation. The too analytical mind, so Kafka may want to imply, is ill-equipped to solve mysteries. Kafka's protagonist is saved and led back into life by an encounter with a hunting dog, that is, one well-versed in the acquisition of food;

---

[6] Werner Hoffmann, *Kafkas Aphorismen* (Bern & Munich: Francke, 1975), p. 9. The quotation reads: "(Seine 'ganze Literatur') hätte eine neue Kabbala werden sollen, eine neue Geheimlehre, die über die Grenzen des Irdischen hinausgeführt hätte in eine höhere geistige Welt."

a successful counterpart — a physically competent dog — to the intellectually inquiring dog, he inspires the despairing researcher to go on with his life and his investigations of the inexplicable, in other words to go on with his attempt to define the ineffable.

In "Forschungen eines Hundes" the protagonist decides to study the source of music, an art form which is capable of establishing a direct relationship between a timeless realm and a time-bound being. One of Kafka's aphorisms, which were arranged by him in sequence and titled "Betrachtungen" by Brod, refers in an oblique way to the situation of a researching (writing) "dog." "He devours the leavings from his own table; thereby he indeed does become fuller than all others for a little while, unlearns, however, how to eat (the food) from the tabletop; as a consequence then, of course, the leavings themselves are no longer available."[8] This brief parable, I should like to propose, once more defines the writer as one who lives like a dog from the scraps of his life. Having forgotten how to nourish himself in the usual way, he gradually declines in the physical sense and thus becomes bereft of the experience which had nourished his artistic sensibilities. But in "Josefine die Sängerin, oder das Volk der Mäuse" the artist is the focus of attention, while the observer, here a representative mouse or non-entity, views her circumspectly from a vantage point in the midst of her audience. The story's tone is propitiatory. The nameless narrator, who regards himself to be a "we" rather than an individual, reconciles his constituency to the artist's great vanity, a necessary evil accompanying the single-mindedness with which she pursues her goal. Hoffmann attributes a similar egotism to Kafka: "He remained an egocentric person, for whom — as he passes judgment on himself — his own salvation was his primary concern."[7] The last words, it would seem, that Kafka wrote were therefore a tribute to his readers (that these would be numbered in the millions in many lands even he could not have imagined, no less anticipated); he absolved them of the guilt acquired by their having been preoccupied with matters of survival and only peripherally aware of his work in bolstering their sense of identity and the meaningfulness of their lives. I should like to suggest that this story also conveys Kafka's giving his blessing to the common people, a blessing to make up for the blessing his father had stubbornly failed to afford him.

However, Kafka depicted the end of his mission not in "Josefine," but in "Der Bau." It like no other one of his works comes closer to

---

[7] Hoffmann, *Kafkas Aphorismen*, p. 95. The quotation reads: "Er blieb ein egozentrischer Mensch, dem es — so urteilt er über sich selbst — zuerst und vor allem auf das eigene Seelenheil ankam."

achieving his goal of promulgating the kind of truth he sought to express in the later years of his life; the narrative strives to turn the art of storytelling into an exercise in putting the ineffable into words, to make a final statement about the purpose and meaningfulness of his writing. The protagonist is at one and the same time a metaphor for Kafka, the earth-bound architect, creator of an elaborate structure which contains, by and large, only emptiness, and an "I," Kafka's concept of his "true" self. In this latter respect, the burrower resembles the depersonalized narrator in "Eine kleine Frau." Tension in "Der Bau," which is perhaps the only one of the elements essential to a work of fiction found in the "story," is created by the narrator's recognition that he exists as a series of dichotomies, in which each part contends with a counterpart. The very structure of "Der Bau" is based on the idea of duality, since it consists of two sections of approximately equal length. In one, the creator of the underground maze lies outside of it as a separate entity. Some reference to gnostic thinking may underlie this representation of the nature of the creative act, since it must be presupposed that that which was once a whole (entirely ineffable) has now become a flawed image of itself. Thus at the beginning of Kafka's survey of his mission, he considers the problem of human error and the writer's fallibility with which he has to deal. Among his aphorisms there is one which definitively describes the dilemma of the writer intent upon expressing the truth. It reads: "Truth is indivisible, can therefore not know itself, (and) must be a lie."[h] The protagonist in "Der Bau," lying outside the burrow's camouflaged entrance, luxuriates in the thought of all he has accomplished, but worries about the enemies he senses are lurking nearby, waiting for an opportunity to attack him by first gaining entry into his work in order to be able to pounce on him. The connotation of this state of affairs is that Kafka's (the writer's) physical being which he has set apart from his work (or vice versa) remains subject to the dangers of ill health, doubts about his ability to achieve his goals, the indifference of others to his mission — in sum, all the predators (problems) which pursue the inhabitants of the natural world. Kafka made this same point succinctly in a letter to Max Brod: "I have not bribed my way out (of all ills) with my writing."[8]

The antagonist, the opponent who exists in almost all of Kafka's stories (and in a multiplicity of forms in the novels) as a physical presence, a being distinct from the protagonist (e.g., the father in the early narratives, the officer of the execution, the groom in "Ein

[8] Kafka, *Briefe 1902-1924*, p. 385. The quotation reads: "Ich habe mich durch das Schreiben nicht losgekauft."

Landarzt," a little woman), has become in "Der Bau" a destructive force within the self. When the burrower finally retreats inside his castle keep which he has constructed as a mighty fortress to withstand the attack of the fiercest enemy (death), he finds that the situation which prevailed on the outside has not changed; he is beset by the same rapacious armies. They surround him even though he has, by diving into the depths of the earth, surrendered to them his physical self. No longer a divided being, he has given up life in the world and turned into a presence shaped by words on a page. He has accomplished this (final) transformation because it becomes for him the ultimate sacrifice that he must make in the name of the cause for which he has lived. The eighty-sixth of his aphorisms portrays his struggle to rise above a dichotomous existence. It argues: "Since the fall of man we have been in essence at the same point in regard to our capacity to know (the difference) between right (good) and wrong (evil); nevertheless, it is precisely here where we seek to assign particular merits to ourselves. But it is only on the other side of (this kind of) knowledge that true distinctions (or dissimilarities) begin. The illusion that this is not so is produced by the following (circumstance): No one can be content with knowledge alone, but must strive to act in accordance with it. However, no one has been given the (needed) strength to do this; one must therefore destroy one's self, even at the (great) risk of even in this way failing to acquire the necessary strength, but no one has another recourse, except to make this last effort (attempt). This is also the meaning of the threat of death which accompanies the injunction against eating of (the fruit) of the tree of knowledge; perhaps this is also the original significance of (the phenomenon of) natural death."[i]

Transferred into a work of fiction, a fable, these philosophic considerations become metaphors which unfold the story. As long as the burrower remains above ground, that is, walks on the earth, the knowledge he has acquired as the result of his having been born a natural creature suffices to the extent that he can deal with transitory problems, for example, the threat to his life and work made by a natural enemy. In other words, this kind of knowledge suffices in the real world. In regard to literature, it would be appropriate to assume that Kafka considered that realistic writing contended well with certain, but not all contingencies. Thus, the burrower's initial judgment about his maze, that it was good, was a reasonable evaluation which Kafka might have produced in viewing his early publications. Once inside his structure, an attempt to build the tower of Babel underground, the "I"-protagonist, having given up his effort to deal with his perplexingly dichotomous situation on the level of diurnal life, nevertheless fails to find his aspirations at an end. He is driven by the imperfections of the burrow and by self-doubt in the form of the enemy within to press on with his work, to make an inroad on the very last frontier, the border between the known (visible) and the unknown (invisible) world. There remains, however, one barrier which the questing animal cannot cross over or find his way through; it is the state of mortality in the physical sense and of culpability in the moral sense into which he (the human being symbolized by the animal protagonist in the latter instance) was born. Since "Der Bau" lacks an ending, there is no resolution to the dilemma faced by the architect-artist. The question of whether or not he has breached the wall between the finite and the infinite or been able to express even indirectly truths that have no referential basis is left unanswered. But in "Der Bau" the question has at least been asked. Although it was apparently not Kafka's intent almost to close his literary career in mid-sentence, the ambiguity with which the fable echoes out is, no doubt, true to human life, even more so than either the catastrophic or the peaceful death of the burrower envisioned by interpreters of the story.[9] The ending which is no ending is, in fact, a most apt metaphor for the relationship between an artist and his work. Both are transient in the world, but, intertwined, continue to exist as a way of knowing life's eternal (immutable) values.[10]

The concept that the expression of truth or truths was the primary concern in literature was not one that Kafka considered debatable. (In this case it is also clear that he did not hold this objective to be the only one he aspired to attain.) In recent times the problematical nature of the assumption that philosophic absolutes such as the pure, the true,

---

[9] Benjamin has made a trenchant comment on ambiguity in Kafka: "Kafka's entire work presents a code of (symbolic) gestures (or movements) which by no means have a clear symbolic significance for the author from the start; rather they solicit (that kind of) significance (by appearing) time and again in different contexts and experimental arrangements." The quotation reads: "Kafkas ganzes Werk (stellt) einen Kodex von Gesten (dar), die keineswegs von Hause aus für den Verfasser eine sichere symbolische Bedeutung haben, vielmehr in immer wieder anderen Zusammenhängen und Versuchsanordnungen um eine solche angegangen werden," Walter Benjamin, *Benjamin über Kafka*, ed. Hermann Schweppenhäuser (Frankfurt am Main: Suhrkamp, 1981), p. 18.

[10] Walter Strauss comments on the relationship between art and the immutable and on this occasion makes use of a symbol from "Der Bau": "Art makes possible the communion with the Indestructible; art offers the individual the freedom to contemplate that inward Truth from which it removes the veils and masks, but which art cannot disclose directly since the language of truth is not the word, but the Word restored to its original silence," Walter A. Strauss, *On the Threshold of a New Kabbalah*, p. 208.

the immutable can be represented in the literary arts has been given close scrutiny. Perhaps one of the most concentrated efforts to establish first a valid relationship between truth and reality and then truth and literature in the twentieth century was made by the philosopher Karl Popper. In essence, Popper posits that there are three realms of actuality or reality, the existence of which can be philosophically established; he uses the term "world" for these areas. In World 1 the presence of physical objects prevails, and the concept of truth applies when there is a correspondence between what the mind perceives and what the world actually contains. The second kind of reality which Popper identifies as World 2 is the province of subjective experience, the conscious experiences of human beings. In World 3 Popper puts what he maintains is "the world of the logical contents of books, libraries, computer memories, and such like."[11] When Popper's postulate is applied to the field of literature and literary criticism, the tendency in recent times, as Louise A. Desalvo has pointed out, has been to try to reach conclusions about the validity of these creative arts by assigning them to World 2. Desalvo contends: "The subjectivist theories currently in vogue usually maintain (a) that a work of literature, because it is written in language (itself a symbol system), cannot possibly say anything about reality or effect changes in reality and/or (b) that a work of literature, because it is filtered through the consciousness of a writer, can tell us nothing about reality; it can tell us only about the consciousness of its author; and/or (c) that a work of literature, because it is experienced by the consciousness of a reader, can tell us nothing about reality or the consciousness of its author — all we can talk about is a reader's response to the work of literature, or of our own response to a work of literature."[12] According to these considerations literature and the study of literature basically belong in the second category of Popper's attempt to deal philosophically with the concept of reality. However, these two literary fields cannot by force of reason be removed either from World 1, since books, essays, and the like exist there as things, or from World 3, since they also exist as a form of knowledge.

The insight provided by emphasizing the subjective nature of the literary arts in relating them to the pursuit of truth leads to an expansion of the concept of their purposefulness. Without eliminating the contention that the element of literalness — art as an imitation of

---

[11] Quoted in T. E. Burke, *The Philosophy of Popper* (Manchester, England: Manchester University Press, 1983), p. 105.

[12] Louise A. Desalvo, "Popper in the Realm of Literary Criticism" in *In Pursuit of Truth*, ed. Paul Levinson (New Jersey: Humanities Press, 1985), p. 185.

life — is an aspect of the work of art, this reevaluation grants greater significance to the insubstantial products of the mind. In regard to the charge that some art, for example, dadaistic art, defiantly resists being identified with any kind of reality, it cannot be refuted that such excursions into the realm of the irrational are per se a reaction to the world as it exists. At the same time, the function of the creative use of the imagination (constructing imaginary gardens with real toads in them, as Marianne Moore's definition of poetry proposes) necessarily acquires greater significance. Desalvo, writing specifically about the literary arts, reaches this conclusion: "Literary creation, although it involves a certain amount of inspiration, is at base a human problem-solving activity directed to the realities of the world."[13]

It is, I propose, quite appropriate to consider Kafka's fiction in this light, although, of course, no direct relationship exists between it and Popper's work. The autobiographical import in all of Kafka's stories, published and unpublished, points unmistakably in the direction of the conclusion that he used his creative abilities to a great degree to solve the problems he encountered in his conflict-ridden life. At first, he sought through his writing to find a remedy for, or, as he called it, a way out of the oppression he believed he was being subjected to by his father and his father's world and to find an end to the depression which the struggle engendered in him. Later he undertook in his work to make his own particular situation the general one, to use his personal problems, even those he encountered as a writer, to illustrate the malaise of humankind in their fallen (culpable) state. In a letter to Max Brod, he characterized himself as the kind of writer who plays the role of the scapegoat: "The definition of an author, an author of this kind, and an explanation of (the exercise of) his influence, if there is an influence at all: He is the scapegoat for humanity, he allows human beings to enjoy their sinning without (feeling) guilt — almost without (feeling) guilt."[14j] The process which the writer Kafka evolved as a means to achieve this catharsis was a matter of establishing the truth of the situation by exposing the non-truth, the lies which conceal it. In Popper's purview the search for truth involves much the same activity; the first part of his statement makes manifest the basis on which the viability of the concept of truth rests. Popper maintains: "The idea of error implies that of truth as the standard of which we may fall short. It implies that, though we may seek for truth, and though we may even find truth (as I believe we do in many cases), we can never be

---

[13] Desalvo, "Popper in the Realm of Literary Criticism," p. 188.

[14] Kafka, *Briefe 1902-1924*, p. 386.

quite certain we have found it. There is always a possibility of error."[15]

A recent addition to the interpretation of Popper's philosophy holds that truth itself is the instrument or instrumentality which brings truth to light. Mario Vargas Llosa asserts: "Truth is, in the first instance, a hypothesis or a theory that attempts to solve a problem."[16] Therefore, whether Kafka rendered his final verdict on the success of his mission as a writer in "Josefine," which contains the last words he wrote, or in "Der Bau," which is undeniably a summation of his literary career, is a moot point. In the former he seems to have reached the conclusion that his mission to promulgate truth has been accomplished. The emperor's messenger has indeed traversed the limitless cosmos and then the multitudinous habitations of the earth and spread abroad the self-knowledge which he was commissioned to unfold; even the last, most humble, and most hidden of all human beings has permitted the message to be whispered in his ear. The ambiguous ending of "Der Bau," however, also has its affirmative aspect, for even the probability that death itself is an ending, portending defeat in the form of an unfinished quest, may be an error in thinking, in Kafka's terminology, a lie, and remains unsubstantiated. In the final analysis the burrower's (Kafka's) inroad on the last frontier between the perceptible and the insubstantial worlds, the real world and the world that enfolds it, can but represent a literary triumph.

[15] Karl Popper, *The Open Society and its Enemies* (London: Routledge & Kegan Paul, 1962, 4th ed.), II, 275.

[16] Mario Vargas Llosa, "Updating Karl Popper," *PMLA*, 105:5 (Oct. 1990), 1018.

Notes

a. "Wenn man doch ein Indianer wäre, gleich bereit, und auf dem rennenden Pferde, schief in der Luft, immer wieder kurz erzitterte über dem zitternden Boden, bis man die Sporen ließ, denn es gab keine Sporen, bis man die Zügel wegwarf, denn es gab keine Zügel, und kaum das Land vor sich als glattgemähte Heide sah, schon ohne Pferdehals und Pferdekopf" (35).

b. "Aus denen kann man ja niemals eine klare Auskunft bekommen.... Diese Gespenster scheinen über ihre Existenz mehr im Zweifel zu sein als wir...." (38).

c. "Nur so kann geschrieben werden, nur in einem solchen Zusammenhang, mit solcher vollständigen Öffnung des Leibes und der Seele."

d. "Vorstellungen wie z.B. die, daß ich ausgestreckt auf dem Boden liege, wie ein Braten zerschnitten bin und ein solches Fleischstück langsam mit der Hand einem Hund in die Ecke zuschiebe — , solche Vorstellungen sind die tägliche Nahrung meines Kopfes."

e. "Nackt, dem Froste dieses unglückseligsten Zeitalters ausgesetzt, mit irdischem Wagen, unirdischen Pferden, treibe ich alter Mann mich umher" (117).

f. "Die Kunst fliegt um die Wahrheit, aber mit der entschiedenen Absicht, sich nicht zu verbrennen. Ihre Fähigkeit besteht darin, in der dunklen Leere einen Ort zu finden, wo der Strahl des Lichts, ohne daß dies vorher zu erkennen gewesen wäre, kräftig aufgefangen werden kann" (H 77).

g. "Er frißt den Abfall vom eigenen Tisch, dadurch wird er zwar ein Weilchen lang satter als alle, verlernt aber, oben vom Tisch zu essen; dadurch hört dann aber auch der Abfall auf" (H 36).

h. "Wahrheit ist unteilbar, kann sich also selbst nicht erkennen, muß Lüge sein" (H 36).

i. "Seit dem Sündenfall sind wir in der Fähigkeit zur Erkenntnis des Guten und Bösen im Wesentlichen gleich; trotzdem suchen wir gerade hier unsere besonderen Vorzüge. Aber erst jenseits dieser Erkenntnis beginnen die wahren Verschiedenheiten. Der gegenteilige Schein wird durch folgendes hervorgerufen: Niemand kann sich mit der Erkenntnis allein begnügen, sondern muß sich bestreben, ihr gemäß zu handeln.

Dazu aber ist ihm die Kraft nicht mitgegeben, er muß daher sich zerstören, selbst auf die Gefahr hin, sogar dadurch die notwendige Kraft nicht zu erhalten, aber es bleibt ihm nichts anderes übrig, als dieser letzte Versuch. (Das ist auch der Sinn der Todesdrohung beim Verbot des Essens vom Baume der Erkenntnis; vielleicht ist das auch der ursprüngliche Sinn des natürlichen Todes") (H 37).

j. "Die Definition des Schriftstellers, eines solchen Schriftstellers, und die Erklärung seiner Wirkung, wenn es eine Wirkung überhaupt gibt: Er ist der Sündenbock der Menschheit, er erlaubt den Menschen, eine Sünde schuldlos zu genießen, fast schuldlos."

Bibliography

I. Primary Sources

Kafka, Franz. *Beschreibung eines Kampfes*. Frankfurt/M: Fischer, 1976. (References to this volume appear in the text in parentheses with the rubric BK.)

_____. *Briefe 1902-1924*. New York: Schocken, 1958.

_____. *Erzählungen*. Frankfurt/M: Fischer, 1976. (References to volume appear in the text in parentheses without a rubric.)

_____. *Hochzeitsvorbereitungen auf dem Lande*. Frankfurt/M: Fischer, 1976. (References to this volume appear in the text in parentheses with the rubric H.)

_____. *Letters to Milena*. Trans. & Intro. Philip Boehm. New York: Schocken, 1990.

_____. *Tagebücher 1910-1923*. Frankfurt/M: Fischer, 1976.

II. Secondary Sources.

Allemann, Beda. "Metaphor and Antimetaphor." In *Interpretation: The Poetry of Meaning*. Ed. Stanley Romaine Hopper and David L. Miller. New York: Harcourt, Brace and World, 1967.

Benjamin, Walter. *Benjamin über Kafka*. Ed. Hermann Schweppenhäuser. Frankfurt/M: Suhrkamp, 1981.

Boulby, Mark. "Kafka's End: A Reassessment of 'The Burrow.'" *The German Quarterly*, 55:2 (March 1982), 175-186.

Burke, T.E. *The Philosophy of Popper*. Manchester, Eng.: Manchester Univ. Press, 1983.

Corngold, Stanley. *Franz Kafka: The Necessity of Form*. Ithaca and London: Cornell Univ. Press, 1988.

Desalvo, Louise A. "Popper in the Realm of Literary Criticism." In *In Pursuit of Truth*. Ed. Paul Levinson. New Jersey: Humanities Press, 1983.

Deutsch, Eliot. *On Truth: An Ontological Theory*. Honolulu: The Univ. Press of Hawaii, 1979.

Emrich, Wilhelm. *Franz Kafka*. Frankfurt/M: Athenäum, 1960.

Fingerhut, Karlheinz. "Die Erzählungen." In *Kafka-Handbuch*. Ed. Hartmut Binder. Stuttgart: Alfred Kröner, 1979.

Gadamer, Hans-Georg. *Truth and Method*. New York: Seabury Press, 1975.

Grimm, Reinhold. "Comparing Kafka and Nietzsche." *The German Quarterly*, 52:3 (May 1979), 339-350.

Gross, Ruth. "Of Mice and Women: Reflections on a Discourse." In *Franz Kafka: His Craft and Thought*. Ed. Roman Struc and J.C. Yardley. Waterloo, Canada: Wilfrid Laurier Univ. Press, 1986.

Guth, Hans P. "Symbol and Contextual Restraint." *PMLA*, 80:411 (Sept. 1965), 427-431.

Hamburger, Käte. *Wahrheit und ästhetische Wahrheit*. Stuttgart: Klett-Cotta, 1979.

Heidsieck, Arnold. "Logic and Ontology in Kafka's Fiction." In *The Dove and the Mole*. Ed. Moshe Lazar and Ronald Gottesman. Malibu: Undena Publications, 1987.

Henel, Heinrich. "Kafka's *Der Bau* or, How to Escape from a Maze." In *The Discontinuous Tradition*. Ed. P.T. Ganz. Oxford: Clarendon Press, 1971.

Henel, Ingeborg. "Das Spätwerk." In *Kafka-Handbuch*. Ed. Hartmut Binder. Stuttgart: Alfred Kröner, 1979.

_____. "Periodisierung und Entwicklung." In *Kafka-Handbuch*. Ed. Hartmut Binder. Stuttgart: Alfred Kröner, 1979.

Hillmann, Heinz. *Franz Kafka: Dichtungstheorie und Dichtungsgestalt*. Bonn: Bouvier/Herbert Grundmann, 1973.

Hoffmann, Werner. *Kafkas Aphorismen*. Bern and Munich: Francke, 1975.

Hofstadter, Albert. *Truth and Art*. New York and London: Columbia Univ. Press, 1965.

Hospers, John. *Meaning and Truth in the Arts.* Chapel Hill: Univ. of North Carolina Press, 1946.

Kafka-Handbuch. Ed. Hartmut Binder. Stuttgart: Alfred Kröner, 1979. 2 vols.

"Kafka's Principal Works and His Recorded Reading." In *Twentieth Century Interpretations of "The Trial."* Ed. James Rolleston. Englewood Cliffs, N.J.: Prentice Hall, 1976.

Kainz, Friedrich. *Aesthetics the Science.* Trans. Herbert M. Schueller. Detroit: Wayne State Univ. Press, 1962.

Karl, Frederick R. *Franz Kafka: Representative Man.* New York: Ticknor and Fields, 1991.

Kayser, Wolfgang. *Die Wahrheit der Dichter.* Hamburg: Rowohlt, 1959.

Llosa, Mario Vargas. "Updating Karl Popper." *PMLA,* 105:5 (Oct. 1990), 1018-1025.

Nagel, Bert. *Franz Kafka.* Berlin: Erich Schmidt, 1974.

Neumann, Gerhard. "Die Arbeit in der Alchimistengäßchen." In *Kafka-Handbuch.* Ed. Hartmut Binder. Stuttgart: Alfred Kröner, 1979.

Pascal, Roy. *Kafka's Narrators.* Cambridge: Cambridge Univ. Press, 1982.

Pasley, Malcolm. "Kafka and the Theme of 'Berufung.'" *Oxford German Studies,* 9 (1978), 139-149.

Politzer, Heinz. *Franz Kafka: Parable and Paradox.* Ithaca, N.Y.: Cornell Univ. Press, 1962.

Pongs, Hermann. *Franz Kafka: Dichter des Labyrinths.* Heidelberg: Wolfgang Rothe, 1960.

Popper, Karl. *The Open Society and its Enemies.* London: Routledge and Kegan Paul, 1962 (4th ed.).

Price, Kingsley B. "Is There Artistic Truth?" In *Contemporary Studies in Aesthetics.* Ed. Francis J. Coleman. New York, etc.: McGraw Hill, 1968.

Ried, Louis Arnaud. "Art, Truth and Reality." In *Aesthetics in the Modern World.* Ed. Harold Osborne. New York: Weybright and Takley, 1968.

Robertson, Ritchie. *Kafka: Judaism, Politics, and Literature.* Oxford: Clarendon Press, 1985.

End of a Mission

Sandbank, Shimon. *After Kafka*. Athens: Univ. of Georgia Press, 1989.

Sokel, Walter H. *Franz Kafka: Tragik und Ironie*. Munich/Vienna: Albert Langen/Georg Müller, 1964.

_____. "Language and Truth in the Two Worlds of Franz Kafka." *The German Quarterly*, 52:3 (May 1979), 364-384.

_____. "Zur Sprachauffassung und Poetik Franz Kafkas." In *Themen und Probleme*. Ed. Claude David. Göttingen: Vandenhoeck & Ruprecht, 1980.

Strauss, Walter A. *On the Threshold of a New Kabbalah*. New York, etc.: Peter Lang, 1988.

Sussman, Henry. *Franz Kafka: Geometrician of Metaphor*. Madison, Wisconsin: Coda Press, 1979.

Thiher, Allen. *Franz Kafka: A Study of the Short Fiction*. Boston: Twayne, 1990.

Weigand, Hermann J. "Franz Kafka's 'The Burrow' ('Der Bau'): An Analytical Essay." *PMLA*, 87:2 (March 1972), 152-165.

Wellek, Rene and Austin Warren. *Theory of Literature*. New York: Harcourt, Brace, 1956.

Winkelmann, John. "Kafka's 'Forschungen eines Hundes.'" *Monatshefte*, 59:3 (Fall 1967), 204-216.

INDEX

Emrich, Wilhelm, 38, 39, 74
"Erstes Leid" ("First Sorrow"/
    "Early Sorrow"), 24-26, 93

Fingerhut, Karlheinz, 75
"First Sorrow," see "Erstes Leid"
"Forschungen eines Hundes"
    ("The Research/ Investigations
    of a Dog"), 31-36, 38, 40, 81,
    93, 95

Gadamer, Hans Georg, 8-10
Garden of Eden, 79, 83, 84
George, Stefan, 5
Glasperlenspiel, Das (*The Glass Bead
    Game*), 35
gnosticism, 78, 97
Goethe, Johann Wolfgang von, 4,
    25
Gottfried von Strassburg, 70
Gregor Samsa ("Die
    Verwandlung"), 3, 16, 32, 45,
    77
Grimm, Reinhold, 6
Gross, Ruth, 56, 58
Guth, Hans P., 19

Heidegger, Martin, 59
Hesse Hermann, 35
Henel, Heinrich, 77n, 79-81
Henel, Ingeborg, 34, 76
Hillmann, Heinz, 25, 31, 53
Hoffmann, Werner, 94, 96
Hofmannsthal, Hugo von, 5, 6
Hofstadter, Albert, 7
"Hunger Artist, A," see "Ein
    Hungerkünstler", 22, 44-46, 48-
    53, 60, 62, 77
Husserl, Edmund, 6

immutability (the immutable), 1,
    4, 5, 7, 8, 10, 22, 28, 41, 50, 60,
    63, 67, 72, 78, 82, 84, 92, 94, 99
impresario, the ("Ein
    Hungerkünstler"), 7, 8, 51, 52;
    ("Erstes Leid"), 24, 25

"In der Srafkolonie" ("In the
    Penal Colony"), 3, 32, 46, 48,
    49, 72-74, 76, 91, 92
"In the Penal Colony," see "In der
    Strafkolonie"
"In the State of Misery," see
    "Unglücklichsein"
"In the Theater-Gallery," see "In
    der Galerie"
Isolde, 70

Janouch, Gustav, 36
Jesenská, Milena, 16n, 44, 66
Job, 36
Josef K. (*Der Prozeß*), 28, 56
Josefine "Josefine, Die Sängerin
    oder Das Volk der Mäuse"
    ("Josefine the Songstress, or
    The Mouse People"), 31, 54,
    56- 58, 60-65, 75, 90, 96, 102
Joseph (Bible), 56
"Judgment, The," see "Urteil,
    Das"

Kafka, Ottla, 64
Kainz, Friedrich, 6
Karl, Frederick R., 19, 21
Kayser, Wolfgang, 7
Keats, John, 5
King Lear, 19
Klopstock, Robert, 38, 66
knowledge, 2, 8, 9, 11, 25, 26, 28,
    33, 36, 39-41, 59, 83, 98, 102

Leiden des jungen Werthers, Die (*The
    Sorrows of Young Werther*), 25
little woman, a ("Eine kleine
    Frau"), 29-31, 97
"Little Woman, A," see "Eine
    kleine Frau"
Llosa, Mario Vargas, 102
Lord Chandos letter, 6

man from the country, the ("Vor
    dem Gesetz"), 28, 29, 53
Mauthner, Fritz, 6
Maximen und Reflektionen, 4

President Roosevelt's library, the heart of the house
at Sagamore Hill, Oyster Bay, N.Y., 1906.

Underwood and Underwood, publishers. LC-DIG-stereo-1802330.
Library of Congress Prints and Photographs Division, Washington, D.C.

Tedie, the scion of the Roosevelt family, age seven.

TRC 520.11-004. Houghton Library, Harvard University.

Tedie Roosevelt, eager to read and fussy about his pen, writing to his father, Philadelphia, September 18, 1872.
MS Am 1454.48 (seq. 74).
Houghton Library,
Harvard University.

Tedie joking with his sister on Darwinian theory, letter to Anna Roosevelt Cowles, Dresden, September 21, 1873.
MS Am 1454.48. Houghton Library,
Harvard University.

Dresden Literary American Club, with the motto W.A.N.A
(We Are No Asses): (*from left*) Theodore, 14; Elliott, 13;
cousin Maud, 12; Corinne, 11; and cousin John, 14; July 1, 1873.
TRC 520.11-006. Houghton Library, Harvard University.

Theodore Roosevelt, dressed for sailing and ready to tell
hunting stories, at Harvard College. TRC 520.11-011.
Houghton Library, Harvard University.

top:
Theodore Roosevelt enjoying a cowboy's life of books and guns and his horse Dakota, 1884.
Library of Congress, Washington, D.C. Image courtesy of the Theodore Roosevelt Center at Dickinson State University and the Library of Congress Prints and Photographs Division, Washington, D.C.

bottom:
Edith Kermit Roosevelt, reading from a favorite book, as she often did aloud with her husband, c. 1902.
Schloss, photographer. LC-DIG-ppmsca-36316. Library of Congress Prints and Photographs Division, Washington, D.C.

Theodore Roosevelt, always with a book in hand
or nearby in his Sagamore Hill library.

R500.R67-003. Houghton Library, Harvard University.

The *Winning of the West* manuscript in Roosevelt's
handwriting with his usual accretions.

Theodore Roosevelt, home from Cuba, crafting *The Rough Riders*
at a makeshift desk in Montauk, Long Island.

R560.3.EL61-017. Houghton Library, Harvard University.

"A square deal for every man, big or small, rich or poor":
President Roosevelt, Lynn, Massachusetts, November 13, 1902.
*Underwood & Underwood, publishers. LC-DIG-stereo-1s01977. Library of Congress
Prints and Photographs Division, Washington, D.C.*

"Next! A president
who 'does' things."
Charles Lewis Bartholomew.
*LC-DIG-ppmsca-37840. Library
of Congress Prints & Photographs,
Washington, D.C.*

Theodore Roosevelt, working on an essay, Sagamore Hill, 1905.
Fawcett Waldon, photographer.

"A Few Shots at the King's English," by Edward Windsor Kemble, September 1906. *Houghton Library, Harvard University.*

President Roosevelt, the outdoorsman, reading with his rescue dog Skip at the West Divide Creek ranch house, Colorado, September 1905. Alexander Lambert, photographer.

LC-DIG-stereo-1s02164. Library of Congress Prints & Photographs, Washington, D.C.

Theodore Roosevelt, in stylish clothes, posing at his desk
in his office at Sagamore Hill, September 11, 1905.
LC-DIG-ppmsca-35996. Library of Congress Prints & Photographs, Washington, D.C.

Roosevelt reading from his Pigskin Library in front of
his tent in a Kenyan hunting camp, April 1910.

LC-DIG-ppmsca-36549. Library of Congress Prints & Photographs, Washington, D.C.

Theodore, in netting and gloves, writing *Through the Brazilian Wilderness*, in
lantern slide of Roosevelt's Brazil expedition, 1913, taken by his son Kermit.
LC-DIG-ds-09857. Library of Congress Prints & Photographs, Washington, D.C.

"Just Luck," by Udo J. Keppler, July 20, 1910.
Published by Keppler and Schwarzmann, Puck Building. LC-DIG-ppmsca-27650.
Library of Congress Prints & Photographs, Washington, D.C.